From the **Netflix** Original Series, *Last Chance U*
BRITTANY WAGNER

NEXT CHANCE YOU

Tools, Tips, and Tough Love for Bringing Your A-Game to Life

Health Communications, Inc.
Boca Raton, Florida

www.hcibooks.com

Library of Congress Cataloging-in-Publication Data

Names: Wagner, Brittany, 1977- author.
Title: Next chance you : tools, tips, and tough love for bringing your
A-game to life / Brittany Wagner.
Description: First Edition. | Boca Raton, FL : Health Communications, Inc.,
2021.
Identifiers: LCCN 2021020556 (print) | LCCN 2021020557 (ebook) | ISBN
9780757324024 (trade paperback) | ISBN 9780757324031 (ebook)
Subjects: LCSH: Self-actualization (Psychology) | Motivation (Psychology) |
Success.
Classification: LCC BF637.S4 W334 2021 (print) | LCC BF637.S4 (ebook) |
DDC 158.1--dc23
LC record available at https://lccn.loc.gov/2021020556
LC ebook record available at https://lccn.loc.gov/2021020557

ISBN-13: 978-0-7573-2402-4 (Paperback)
ISBN-10: 07573-2402-9 (Paperback)
ISBN-13: 978-0-7573-2403-1 (ePub)
ISBN-10: 07573-2403-7 (ePub)

Publisher: Health Communications, Inc.
1700 NW 2nd Avenue
Boca Raton, FL 33432-1653

Cover photo by Ginnard Archibald
Author photo styling by Randall Porter
Author wardrobe by Billy Reid

Cover and interior design by Larissa Hise Henoch
Interior formatting by Lawna Patterson Oldfield

Praise for *Next Chance You*

"Brittany Wagner stood out on *Last Chance U* because she passionately fought for the student-athletes she counseled—not just to make grades to maintain eligibility, but to carve a path for a successful life after their playing days were over. She genuinely cares about them as people. Years later, they will tell you that they are better for having known her. In her book *Next Chance You*, she brings the same grit and determination to help you live your best life."

—**MICHAEL STRAHAN,** co-host, *Good Morning America*; analyst, *Fox NFL Sunday*; Pro Football Hall of Famer

"When I saw Brittany Wagner share her unique blend of practical advice and tough love to the student-athletes on *Last Chance U,* I could tell that she genuinely cared for and believed in them, even if they had lost faith in themselves. I've since gotten to know her and can tell you that she is the real deal. *Next Chance You,* her blueprint for creating a growth mindset, will empower you, encouraging you to put your best foot forward and take advantage of opportunities that come your way."

—**COURTENEY COX,** actress, producer, and director

"*Next Chance You* is a book chock-full of helpful tips and strategies to help you reach your goals! Brittany and I grew up together in small town Mississippi, and even back then she was learning ways to empower herself and achieve her goals. This book takes her expertise and makes it understandable for people of all ages!"

—**LANCE BASS,** pop icon

"I don't know where I would be today if it wasn't for Brittany Wagner's guidance and endless support. She was a great academic advisor and, maybe even more importantly, she was a life advisor. As a lost twenty-year-old who had made many mistakes in my life, there were days I was alone, with no one to talk to, but she was always there for me with a listening ear and an open heart. Ms. Brittany was not there just to collect a paycheck. She was genuine and truly wanted to help me be the best student and best person I could possibly be. I will never forget the conversations we had that allowed me to learn and grow into the man I am today."

—**DAKOTA ALLEN,** Jacksonville Jaguars linebacker

"Everyone should have someone like Brittany Wagner tutor them through life. Someone who'll take a complicated algebra problem or a life problem and break it down into solvable parts. Someone who'll listen to the first draft of your English essay and gently point out places where it could be improved while simultaneously making you feel as though you're a better writer than you think you are. Someone who'll listen to your deepest aspirations; your most private fears and failures without judgment and with generous portions of kindness and patience—with her signature standard of leaving you better than she found you. Brittany is a fine human during a time in which humanity is in short supply. She can't physically be everywhere for everyone, so this book is the next best thing."

—**GREG WHITELEY,** producer of *Last Chance U*

"Brittany Wagner is so inspiring to me, and with *Next Chance You* she's captured many of her empowering pieces of advice in one place. Anyone who could use a little motivation or help getting themselves on track to create a better life should read this book!"

—**SARA EVANS,** country music star

"Brittany Wagner is the ultimate motivator. She has turned countless people's lives around, including her own, with her brains and her heart. Her legendary tenacity will be portrayed by Courteney Cox in the Hollywood version, but her real-life story is even more riveting to discover. And she's sharing her secrets in *Next Chance You.* The determined single mom has more surrogate 'kids' running around. Brittany can help us all redefine success, both on and off the football field. From the humble East Mississippi Community College football program to Netflix stardom, Brittany maintains a clear-eyed view of what's real and what's hype. *Next Chance You* is a manifesto for living your best life . . . by first believing in yourself."

—**JUJU CHANG,** co-anchor, ABC News *Nightline*

"There is no quick fix in the game of life. It takes blood, sweat, and tears to make our dreams a reality. Brittany Wagner understands this and teaches you how to make your life a success story in *Next Chance You.* She will teach you how to keep pushing toward the success you want, because all dreams can become realities with the right attitude and perseverance."

—**JAMES CONNER,** NFL running back for the Arizona Cardinals and author of *Fear Is a Choice*

To my daughter, Kennedy

All my chances led me to you, my greatest accomplishment.
Thank you for showing me the value in showing up as a single mom.

Contents

Contents

Acknowledgments

No one would even know who I am without Drew Jubera telling Netflix they didn't have a show without me. Thank you, Drew, for seeing the value and humor in this mama duck and her ducklings. More than that, thank you for your friendship.

HCI. The place that I fit into. Christine Belleris, who listened to her son, Nick, and watched a TV show about a football team, and then never wavered on wanting to publish this book. The way in which you were sold that this was going to be great—sold me—at times. Larissa Henoch and Lindsey Mach and the rest of the staff at Health Communications, Inc.—Indebted. Thank you.

My literary agent, Reiko Davis, and the others at Defiore and Company. Unparalleled times to say the least, but we did it! I could not have done this without your guidance, support, and representation.

Cassie Hanjian. You believed in my story, wisdom, and ability long before I did. The loyalty and grit you showed through this process was unmatched. Thank you for knowing me better than I knew myself.

Suzanne Gosselin. Wow! No way can I copy and paste a scripted statement here. You rock! Your words, your style, your organizational skills, the gentle way in which you would say, "Give me more" or "This is crap"—Unbelievable. Mad respect! Thank you! Thank you! Thank you!

This cover is beautiful because of Ginnard Archibald and Randall Porter. Thank you also to Billy Reid, Basic and Asthetik.

Thank you to everyone who made the recorded version of this possible! Ben and the rest of the team at Recorded Books, you rock! I was so nervous about reading this book in a way that the listeners would love it and you made it super easy and fun! Van and the rest of you at Boutwell Studios in Homewood, Alabama, what a blessing to have professionals like you right down the street! Thank you!

The producer of *Last Chance U,* Greg Whiteley, without whom none of this would be possible. Thank you for everything—literally. It was a family effort, I know, so thank you to Erin, Henry, and Scout for sharing your husband and father with those of us all the way in Mississippi.

Jason Arnot, Luke Lorentzen, Alex Auvenshine, Terry Zumalt, Adam Ridley, Gabriel Patay, and the rest of the *Last Chance U* team who made me extremely nervous on day one but by day seven felt like family. Seriously, being around you daily was so much fun. The way you captured my job, my voice, my facial expressions, my fingernails, my space, and then edited it into perfection is beyond amazing to me. I love you all!

East Mississippi Community College and Dr. Rick Young for giving me the opportunity of a lifetime, and by that I am not talking about a Netflix show. I will never forget the faculty, staff, and students with whom I worked for eight years. I am truly better for having been there. Go Lions!

CAA and my agent, Tom Young. Pretty sure I am your most

insignificant client, and yet you still answer my phone calls.

Michael Strahan and SMAC Entertainment. There is quite possibly nothing better than having you on my team. You are great people and that is more important to me than being great business people. Thank you for believing in me!

Courteney Cox. Years of dialect school to help you rid yourself of that Southern accent, and here you go deciding to play me! I cannot wait to hear your version of "Do you have a pencil?" and I am beyond honored that you chose this role. From one single mom to another— nothing but love and xoxo!

Matt Hottle, the brains behind 10 Thousand Pencils, LLC. The reason it exists. We are a perfect balance of "yes" and "no" and without you, I would probably be homeless! I am pretty sure there has not been one single day where you did not believe I could do it. That has kept me going. Thank you! Jason Hutson, the initial logo maker and website designer. I gave you a utensil and a color and you created a brand. Chris Davis, you talked about Star Wars over a bottle of wine and next thing I knew, I had a brand-new website. Thank you for creating, fixing, pivoting, and keeping it all accessible and running for the world to see.

All the athletes I have worked with over the course of my career— you did this! You are the reason I am the person I am today. You are the reason I have had the success I have. I went into this profession thinking I would change you, and I came out changed because of you. Your teamwork, strength, perseverance, wit, smiles, and overall outlook on life is something I aspire to daily.

Quinton Dial, Brandon Lewis, Pat Shed, CJ Odom, Denico Autry, Damien Jacobs, Za'Darius Smith, AJ Stamps, Jarran Reed, Hamp Glover, Christian Russell, Brandon Bell, Lacolton Bester, Fred Tate,

Rodney Davis, Dante Sawyer, Bo Wallace, Chad Kelly, Allen Senti-more, Avery Gennessy, DJ Pettway, Jacquez Johnson, DJ Jordan, and all the rest of you who came before LCU—Your show was equally as amazing!

Ronald Ollie, John Franklin, Wyatt Roberts, Dakota Allen, Chauncey Rivers, Isaiah Wright, DJ Law, James Davis, Diamante Pounds, Tim Bonner, Deandre Johnson, Kam Carter, and the coaches—we had no idea what we were doing or how to do it, but we made a masterpiece just being ourselves. In going through that together, we formed a bond that can never be broken.

Randall Mackey and Ronald Ollie. You two will never know the impact you have had on my life. You stand alone.

My home state of Mississippi. I wish the rest of the world could see you through my eyes. You are generous, rich, diverse, genuine, con-flicted, hardworking, and lovely. Removing the negative labels and growing with every chance. You can do hard things!

My hometown, Clinton. Small, but wise. I had no idea (at the time) the work that went into building a segregated, diverse, funded school system. To those who made the decision to make the Clinton Public School System a priority, you deserve massive kudos. I also had no idea the impact these people and this decision would make on my life. I am extremely grateful to have been raised in this town and to be a Clinton Arrow! Teachers of impact are crucial. Mrs. Jackson, Mrs. King, Mrs. Sholar, Mrs. Edwards, Mrs. Hunt, Mrs. Seagrove, Mrs. Bacon, Mrs. Saul, Mrs. Moorer, Mr. Fehr, Mrs. Simmons, Mrs. Reyn-olds, Ms. Clemons, Mrs. Kyzar—you were some of mine. You made a difference.

Mississippi State University. You gave me my start in more ways than one. David Rosinski and Joe Dier for giving me an opportunity as a student to work in an SEC Media Relations Department. Man, I could run some stat sheets as good as anyone! Ray Berryhill for hiring me as a graduate assistant in the Athletic Academic Office at MSU. A department I didn't even know existed. Ann Carr for mentoring me, teaching me everything I know, and proving to me that a woman (and a single mom) can be solid and successful professionally while also raising a solid and successful daughter. And also, that females can do anything a man can do. To David Ridpath, for making me think logically and believing I was smart. To Pat McMahon and Sylvester Croom for modeling what a head coach should be. I was paying attention. Hail State!

David. Your wisdom and self-awareness are inspirational. I have grown exponentially since having you in my life. I wish you peace, continued happiness, and love. I will always love you. You are enough!

Mark, the meaning and purpose behind all of it is her. For that, I am forever grateful.

Bridget McCart, Richard Shapley, Josh Brackin, Laura Garrett, Lynn Hale, and Charlotte Ann Adams. The circle is small but powerful. Thank you for being in it.

My family—Sheila Wagner; Karley and Abby Weigel; Stafford and Johnnie Lou Marshall; Kent and Kelli Marshall; John, Faith, and Hope Marshall; Bill and Mary Ann Averitt. Proud to be your stepdaughter, aunt, niece, and cousin. I love you all very much!

Those who are gone but not forgotten: Grandmama and Grandaddy (Johnny and Blanche Wagner); Daddy Charles (Charles Roper); and Nana and Papa (Keith and Dorothy Herring)—I wish you were here to see all of this! That hyper, loudmouthed granddaughter of yours did something. But I never could stand by a tree and act like a carrot! Thank goodness for that, huh?! I love you and miss you.

My lifelong soul sisters, Tiffany Kopfinger, Brandi Myers, and Nicole Register. There isn't a story I could tell that you three haven't lived with me. When I think about the span and depth of our friendship, I am completely overwhelmed with gratitude and love. This foursome is the definition of loyalty and unconditional love, and I think we have just scratched the surface. I could not, and more importantly, would not want to do this life without you. My soul mates!

Mom. The woman behind whom I watched juggling it all. A successful, working mom with a very emotionally demanding job, and raising two teenage daughters who could not have been any different. I watched your independence, strength, and determination with admiration. And you have not stopped. I can never repay you for packing up your life and moving with me in order for me to pursue my dreams while raising my daughter. You are my lifesaver and Kennedy's light. I love you!

Dad. The kindest, most tolerant and loving person I know. You taught me invaluable life lessons without me knowing I was learning a dang thing. Your awareness and concern for others is one of the most admirable traits I have ever seen exhibited in any human. Somehow, through osmosis, I received one-tenth of that from you. My greatest quality is loyalty, again, modeled to me by you. Your commitment to living your life is amazing. You committed to running and now have run 70,709.85 miles over your lifespan. You committed to a profession and have changed countless people's lives through practicing and teaching your knowledge. Your family, your friends, your community, your God, and yourself. I will forever be in search of another man to be half the man you are. I love you!

Carolyn. My big sister. You tolerated me—the obnoxious younger sister who always stole your spotlight. So many times your accomplishments, struggles, needs, and just your quiet personality were overlooked or dismissed by my loud, overbearing, in-your-face shit. And yet, you still seem to like me. I don't know how. That speaks to the person you are. There is no one else I would pick to be my sister. Thank you for being my ride or die! I love you.

Kennedy. How did I ever deserve the soul you are? You are my perfect match. You balance me like no other human ever has. Even at twelve years old, I look at you and think, what a wonderful human! I feel sure therapy is in your future due to the countless mistakes I have made in raising you; however, I hope I have also taught you that mistakes are okay . . . and so is therapy! Thank you for understanding (or at least acting like you do) your mom's life, profession, and demands. Your ability to go with the flow and roll with life is inspiring. Please remember: you are always exactly where you need to be; there is a Being bigger than you; and to have faith in, trust, and love the process. Whatever you do little girl, LIVE. Believe in yourself and the opportunities you can create. Ride the roller coasters, climb the ropes course, dive into the ocean, sing made-up songs, and aggressively attack the goal! You are amazing! I love you!

. . . And . . . You. The Fans, Media, Schools, Colleges and Universities, Corporations, and Organizations that have followed me, supported me, and hired me. Your support and generosity is inspirational and has repeatedly given me the confidence to accomplish dreams I didn't even know I had. Thank you—and to you I am forever grateful!

Introduction

Have you ever heard the quote, "Everyone is fighting a battle you know nothing about"? We are all struggling with something in our lives at this very moment, even if that struggle changes a little day-to-day. We might be facing difficulties in our marriage, a setback in our careers, a family dispute, or even a serious health condition. There are times in life when we all get stuck and desperately need a do-over or a second chance to prove, if only to ourselves, that we have what it takes to be great.

As an academic counselor to some of the country's top athletes at East Mississippi Community College (EMCC), I was surrounded by student athletes battling for their second chances every day. They came there for different reasons: poor grades, behavioral issues, run-ins with the law. But at the end of the day, they all had the same goal in mind: their chance at redemption. At success. At a way out. I came there to build something. To help build a program from the ground up, but really to build better people. I came there to change lives; to help these athletes become better versions of themselves, and carve out a better path for their future. The funny thing is, even though I wouldn't admit it to myself until much later, I was also looking for my second chance alongside theirs—a chance to be better because of my experiences instead of becoming bitter; a chance to break out of the excuse mindset and actively create a change in my life and career; a chance to provide bigger and better opportunities for myself and my daughter, Kennedy. Maybe fate put me on this parallel path. Or maybe part of it was that we often attract to our own lives what we are focused on, and what we are throwing out into the universe. I had been focused on my brokenness and acting like a victim. Therefore, I was attracted to a place where I would be surrounded by broken-ness and victims. I would not allow myself to sink into that dark hole only because I had to be strong enough to fight for the others. All the while, the "others" would teach me how to save myself.

While the work I did at EMCC was some of the most important I would ever be part of, I also recognized that when my chance came, I needed to be ready for it. It was only after I engaged in the hard work of changing myself and my mindset from the inside out that my next chance opportunity came to me in the form of a phone call from a Hollywood producer, wanting to film me for a new show called *Last Chance U* on Netflix. While I was not part of the original show idea, I was added in afterward. This was a fortuitous addition. The show became a runaway hit and ultimately gave me a platform—and a sec-ond chance—to pursue a new path and make an even bigger impact on this world.

It wasn't easy, and it wasn't a given. *Last Chance U* was Netflix's first original sports documentary series, and we had no idea if it would resonate or not.

The show came about because of a feature story that *GQ Magazine* published in 2014. They sent freelance writer Drew Jubera to East

Mississippi Community College's campus to follow our football program. Although one of the most successful in the country, producing a slew of players who went on to the NFL, junior college programs were the least well known among the public. Though the feature story that appeared in the magazine was only about four pages long, Drew spent six months in tiny Scooba, population just barely over 700, often in my office and on the sidelines during the team's football practices and games. Other than my small hometown newspaper, I had never been written about before. *GQ* even flew in a photographer to do a photo shoot of the team. It was incredible! I called my mom, dad, sister, and all my friends. "The November issue, you have to go get it the day it comes out," I told them.

November rolled around and I drove to Books-A-Million with a huge smile on my face. I was going to buy every copy the store had in stock. Matthew McConaughey was on the front cover — even better! I grabbed the issue and sat down on the floor, flipping to find our story. There it was! But I couldn't find a mention of me anywhere. *Well, that's disappointing,* I thought. I felt ignored, irrelevant, and mortified that I had bragged to my family and friends. I bought one copy and quietly walked out of the store.

By the time Netflix called about five months later, I was convinced that I wasn't an important member of the team or the football

Gathering with my family for a private watch party for the premier of *Last Chance U.*

On the sidelines before kickoff of an EMCC football game.

program. Ironically, it was Drew Jubera who told the *Last Chance U* producer that Netflix didn't have a show without me. Apparently, he'd written a rather lengthy section about my work as the athletic academic counselor that *GQ* had cut.

I spent fifteen years working with college athletes. I coached them on how to be successful in the classroom, which in turn kept them eligible to play on the field or court. But I learned the hard way that academic issues were almost never about academics. As it turns out, athletes with superhuman abilities are, like the rest of us, mere mortals. Like us, they are also a product of their experiences, environments, and deeply held beliefs about themselves.

At EMCC, we got the players no one else wanted. The guys who weren't good enough in the classroom to go straight to the four-year powerhouse programs. The guys who were incredibly talented but couldn't manage the pressure of the big-time program. The guys who failed drug tests, got arrested, cussed out a coach, or were caught on video punching someone in a bar. The players whose names run across the ticker of ESPN on any given weekend.

I saw my job as a counselor as bigger than "crisis management" or "eligibility maintenance." The young men I counseled didn't start out with a level playing field, and they had much to overcome: the neighborhood they grew up in, voices from the past that told them they weren't smart enough to go to college, the negative self-talk that played on a loop in their heads, and the pressure to perform in front of a very demanding crowd who expected them to shake off injuries, score touchdowns, make tackles, and always win. And somehow, I had to help the players make their second chances work.

As much as I wanted to change their lives, in reality they were changing mine. I loved their stories and their determination and drive. I loved how sometimes they wanted to give up because it was hard, but very few of them did. I loved how they could smile through almost anything.

Those athletes prepared me for a lot; yet nothing could have prepared me for what happened after the first season of *Last Chance U* was released — the outpouring of love from viewers near and far; the articles that identified me as the heartbeat of the series; the phone

Filming an episode of *Last Chance U*.

calls, messages, and tweets I received from the likes of Reese Wither-spoon, Dax Shepard, Kristen Bell, Ricky Gervais, and Snoop Dogg.

While my next chance was, admittedly, a *tad* dramatic, I had to put in the hard work up front so that I could seize the opportunity when it came. I'm still a work in progress, and I still wake up every day to my next chance. A new opportunity to be better and do better than the day before. You do, too. Life isn't a one-shot deal. We aren't working on our last chance, but our next chance. We don't have the opportu-nity for only last chances, but *many* chances to get it right. We're on this Earth to learn to be our best selves, one chance at a time. Every day we are alive is Next Chance *You*. While most second chances in life require a massive amount of patience, perseverance, and persis-tence, we can prepare for these openings each day by cultivating the habits, mindset, and skills required to capitalize on the opportunities that come our way. We can invest in our growth and lean into our best selves in anticipation of our big breaks, maybe even attracting those opportunities in the process. When we make mistakes, we can choose to learn from them and start fresh the next day instead of letting our errors hang over us. When we shift our mindset to one of openness, evolution, and curiosity, we come to see that we can start over at any point, and that every day can truly be a new lease on life.

In the pages of *Next Chance You*, you will find inspiration, practi-cal tools, and real stories designed to help empower you along life's journey. Filled with what came to be known on *Last Chance U* as my signature tough love and practical truth, this book will help every-one—no matter your background, circumstance, or level of educa-tion—find the secret ingredient inside you to make every day count.

When I left Scooba, Mississippi, to launch my own company, 10 Thousand Pencils (10KP), I realized there are persevering athletes like Ronald Ollie and Dakota Allen everywhere; people who have had a difficult hand dealt to them, or maybe brought problems on themselves, but have a fighting spirit that just needs direction and a little lift. We have all faced a second-chance opportunity at some point in our lives. The longer I've observed, the more certain I am that each of us wakes up every single day with a new opportunity to be better than the day before.

Every day is your next chance.

With Kennedy at a *Last Chance U* press event in Los Angeles.

CHAPTER 1
Show Up. Be Present.

"The art of life is to live in the present moment!"
—EMMET FOX

Thanks to Netflix, I am the most well-known guidance counselor or academic advisor in the world. Literally. That means I am super intelligent, right? I must have breezed right through my schooling with straight A's, always doing exactly what I was supposed to do. Academics must have come naturally to me, and I likely loved every second of my education, right?

Nope. That was my older sister, not me. I struggled in school. My studies were neither fun nor easy for me—ever. I am a rule follower. So I did, by nature, tend to comply with people's expectations of me. I distinctly remember when "following the rules" became a challenge. During my sophomore year of college, I transferred from a small private university with a tough academic curriculum to a large public state school in order to take advantage of what I'd hastily decided was my major. The rules changed—along with the stadium size and football talent.

At the private school, my professors had taken attendance and mailed each student's absences home to their parents. My dad had given me my very own attendance lecture at the beginning of the fall semester. Dr. Buddy Wagner had done the math and calculated how much each individual class was costing him. He told me I could miss as many classes as I wanted, but I would be responsible for paying him back the "per class fee." It was not a small number, and I never skipped class again while attending that institution.

The next year, when I arrived at my athletics-loving, public state school, they didn't give a flying flip if I went to class and my dad had no idea what I was up to. Nearly 300 students attended my Chemistry 101 class, and nobody gave a shit if I was one of them. I never went to that class. I remember calling my mom and preparing her for the D grade I knew I was going to make. I had tons of excuses and the truth was not in a single one of them.

The irony is not lost on me that in my role as an athletic academic counselor, one of my primary responsibilities was to convince struggling students with mounds of athletic ability to simply attend their classes. It was, in fact, the first rule I put into place.

"GO TO CLASS!" I pleaded with them at the beginning of every semester. "You will not make the best grade possible in a class you do not attend." East Mississippi Community College had a strict attendance policy: Students were allowed only four unexcused absences in each class. On the fifth absence, they were automatically dropped from the class—no questions asked, no excuses heard.

"Starting today, I am going to monitor your every move," I informed the 200 student-athletes sitting in front of me at our very first academic team meeting. "I will know when you skip class, when you are late to class, when you sleep in class. We may do nothing else, but we will go to class! You know why? Because no matter where you came from, how much money you have, what your ACT score is, or how many tackles or touchdowns you have on the field, every single one of you can show up and be where you say you're going to be. Showing up is not dependent on any level of intelligence or social status, but upon your own effort and determination. We will all show up!"

Learning Doesn't Stop After Graduation

I believe education is much more than curriculum. Our educational journey is the process and experience that most closely mirrors the reality of being a successful adult. The lessons we learn (or don't learn) throughout our school years will deeply impact how we behave as adults and contributing members of society. Through education, we learn social norms—how to respect authority, how to get along with others, how to commit and persevere. We learn discipline, structure, and adaptability. We learn how to pay attention, listen, think critically, and ask for help. While chemical formulas and comma placement are important, they ultimately take a backseat to the life lessons we learn along the way.

One of the biggest lessons is that life requires us to show up. Living has an attendance policy that is standard for everyone. It doesn't matter what neighborhood you live in, what job title you carry, how attractive you are, or what your IQ score is—we all have the ability to show up for our own lives at minimum: to honor our commitments and be where we say we are going to be. There are no excused absences when it comes to living, and we cannot live our best lives if we refuse to show up for them.

Step back for a minute and compartmentalize your life. I imagine wicker baskets with labels on the front of them. (That would be my organizational OCD kicking in.) Each basket represents an area of our lives. What labels make up your life? Here are mine: relationships, work, home responsibilities, self-care, and fun. These are the areas of my life that comprise my entire existence. Some are easier to show up for than others.

As we think about this concept of "showing up," I'm sure many of us are patting ourselves on the back because we passed this first test. *I show up,* we think. *I am dedicated to my job and go to work every single day. I have hardly taken any sick or personal days. I get there early and I stay late. Check! I show up!* But what about the other areas? They are all connected. We don't get to just show up for the areas we like, or those that come easily. Just like school, we don't get to show up for PE and skip chemistry. We must show up for all classes—for all areas of our lives.

Football players are never late to practice. If they are, they face consequences. If practice starts at 3:30 PM, then everyone on the team knows to show up at 2:30. There is routine and ritual—locker-room banter, ankle taping, stretching, mental preparation, and the walk to the field. It is a *process.* You show up early and by 3:30, everyone is on the field, mentally and physically ready to go.

I am always amazed by the fact that not one single junior college football player would "forget" about football practice or oversleep and show up when it was half over or simply not feel like going. When it came to football, they knew how to manage their time and be responsible. But when it came to class, they had absolutely no clue what an alarm clock was, how to tell time, or how to walk across the street. We tend to show up for what we like, what we are good at, or what is easy while making excuses about why we can't show up for what we don't like, what we struggle with, or what we simply don't deem worthwhile.

Showing up for our lives starts with our attitude. Consider the message a habitual class-skipper is sending his teacher: "Hey, Dr. Whatever-Your-Name-Is, I know you went to school for a long time and paid a lot of money to earn multiple degrees so you would be qualified to stand in front of a younger generation and empower them. I know you read and researched and prepared for this class. I know you do all this work so that I can maybe have a brighter future. But I don't care. I don't have enough respect for you or the subject matter to wake up, walk over here, sit still, and give you my attention for fifty minutes."

Those words are extreme, but I have found that they are essentially the attitude a student is taking on when he or she cannot even commit to the bare minimum. Let's think about the people or things in *our lives* we broadcast this message to:

The friend who's going through a hard time that we don't check in on because we think we won't have the "right" words.

The dying relationship we numbly suffer through instead of having the hard conversations.

The health concern we ignore because actually doing something about it would be inconvenient or costly.

The job promotion we never go for because we don't trust in our own strengths and abilities.

Such attitudes may be a sign that we feel inadequate to face the challenges in our lives head-on, or we lack the confidence to solve the problems we encounter. We blame the "teacher" or outward factors for our failure in this area. The hard truth is, it's not the teacher or the "thing"—it's us!

Due to the deficiency within ourselves, we don't allow ourselves to be truly present—or to truly "show up" for that area of our life. It becomes a vicious cycle. Due to our internal struggle, we push away from this one particular area; because we push away, the difficulty grows and we become less and less present in it. This cycle becomes even more complicated when we show up without dealing with the deficiency. When we force ourselves to show up without doing the work, our efforts become a disingenuous performance that takes us out of balance and away from who we are. In my experiences, the only way to truly solve the problem is to do the work. Do the work to fill in the gap of the deficiency, and then show up with genuine emotion and genuine effort.

Let me flip this back to the classroom. In education, I label this as the "Symptom Versus Issue" scenario. I found during my time working with student-athletes, that we often treat the symptom and ignore the root issue. In fact, academic issues are rarely about intelligence and behavior problems. They are almost always the result of root issues that take real work to address.

I had a six-foot-five defensive lineman who constantly got in trouble in math class. The twenty-year-old had already failed intermediate algebra twice. This class was a prerequisite for college algebra, and he had to pass college algebra to graduate and transfer to play Division I football. He had tons of scholarship offers to play at the next level, and those offers were the key to his future.

This math class was vital, but he kept getting in trouble for skipping class, walking out of class, cussing out the teacher, and flipping his desk over. He and I had seen the inside of the dean's office one too many times, and the college was ready to expel him for his behavior issues. That's when I had a realization. He only had behavior problems in math class. Around that time, the young man stormed into my office angry and ready to quit.

He plopped down on the oversized chair and said, "I can't do it. I'm quitting. I just took the first test for the third time and I failed it again. I have no idea what's going on in this class, and everyone else knows exactly what she is talking about. School isn't for me."

Because I had already connected the dots, I knew there was a deficiency for this young man when it came to math. As we talked, I discovered the problem: He had never learned to divide. Here he sat in a college classroom with no concept of division. In order to not feel the anxiety of being embarrassed or found out, he acted out in order to be removed from the situation. His methods had to become more severe and offensive as the teachers would learn to tolerate him, began to like him, or realize what a great football player he was.

Everyone had focused on the behavior—the symptom—but no one had done the work to discover and solve the underlying issue. I encouraged him to show up for this area of his life, even though it meant applying himself to learn something that was difficult for him. He needed to tackle the extra work with determination to grow. He also needed to admit the deficiency in a way that eliminated shame, thus eliminating the symptom—his behavior. A tutor taught the young man division, he passed his classes, played Division I football, graduated (after passing statistics!), and now plays professional football backed up with a college degree. It's amazing to think he was two seconds away from being kicked out of college forever.

Can you relate? Are there deficiencies in your life where you are unwilling to treat the issue and instead find yourself spinning aimlessly on a wheel of chaos, stress, and hopelessness? There is hope. Show up!

Be Where Your Feet Are

I am not the most intelligent person on this Earth, but I do have common sense. And common sense tells me that when I go out to dinner and repeatedly see an entire table of people staring into their phones, we are not showing up for our relationships. When the divorce rate in America is higher than 50 percent and skyrockets during a quarantine, we are clearly struggling in that area.

One night, I was dining at an upscale Mexican restaurant in Birmingham, Alabama, where I now reside. The host seated a middle-aged couple near me. After ordering drinks and an appetizer, they proceeded to each pull out an iPad and give their entire devotion to their screens. I didn't snoop enough to see what they were actually doing, but what they were *not* doing was interacting with each other. I kept waiting for them to stop and talk, but it never happened. I'm sure a series of steps led them to this point of ignoring their partner, but here they sat not showing up at all for each other. And they're not the only ones.

On a trip to speak at a university in Baltimore, Maryland, I noticed bright stickers on the sidewalk below. Spaced about six feet apart, each sticker read, "Safe Walking. Look Up!" I was confused at first. *Why are these stickers here?* I thought. *Why do I need to be concentrating on walking safely? Are the sidewalks about to move? Why do I need a reminder to look up?*

Then I looked around. I watched the hundreds of college students on campus walk past. Every single one of them was looking down at his or her phone as they walked by. They clearly did need the reminder of how to walk responsibly. Before cell phones and social media, it was much easier to just be where our feet are. We were better at living in the present moment before we had reminders of where we were a year ago and constant photos, captions, and notifications urging us to draw comparisons to our peers. My profound, big advice for being present is simply this: Put your phone down, and *be* where your feet (or seat) are.

When we are able to focus fully on the present moment, we can see more clearly the *actual* possibilities in front of us. We can discern between pie-in-the-sky dreams and real opportunities. We can identify the things we have control over versus those we can't control. Accepting the reality of this very moment brings empowerment. When we show up to our lives day after day, living in the present, that daily awareness adds up, pushing us toward amazing possibilities and next chances.

But we can't live in the present moment if we operate from a place of comparison. We cannot be looking backward and moving forward at the same time. And we also cannot be living so far ahead—in an unrealistic wish list of future fairy tales—if we have our feet firmly planted in an appreciation of the now. Just because something bad happened to me in the past doesn't mean I have to attach that fear to my present circumstances. Instead of worrying about what *could* happen, I need to be present in what I am experiencing in this very moment.

Be Present and Be Honest

Comparison is another way we escape our present moment. Iyanla Vanzant wrote, "Comparison is an act of violence against the self." Comparison is false advertisement where we compare another's best to our worst. Not only is it unfair, it's also inaccurate because it's not where my feet are right now. When we compare ourselves to others, we choose to believe something other than reality. I choose to believe I can somehow look like that airbrushed model on the pages of the magazine (or even a girlfriend who I think looks better than me). When I focus on these thoughts, I'm not viewing my life (or the lives of others) transparently. I'm not being honest with myself.

This lack of honesty creates blind spots. I have a newer Infiniti SUV. Something I love in newer models of vehicles is the "safe driving" feature. My car will beep at me if I'm swerving over into the next lane, and nearly slam on the brakes if I am about to hit something. It also has blind-spot sensors. Red, blinking lights on the side mirrors flash when there's a vehicle in my blind spot, warning me to look again and proceed with caution. I think many of us, me included, could use blind-spot flashers in our lives. A way for the universe to signal us to pause, take a second look, and proceed with caution. Those blinking lights could prompt us to be honest with ourselves and where we are. Are we seeing the full picture? Uncovering blind spots can hurt. Sometimes we don't want to face the truth, or even want to know what is real. Facing reality means I have to either accept something or do something to change it.

After my divorce, I struggled to find love again. I dated quite a bit, but I could not find anyone I wanted to be with. Then I met Travis. We met by chance and he lived in the city I was moving to. There was an immediate connection and attraction, and, all of a sudden, I was all in. We dated for over three years. I showed up in a big way for this relationship. I was able to show a level of compassion and understanding I had not been mature enough to show in previous relationships. I was loyal and refused to give up on this man. I saw something in him that he wasn't able to see in himself.

But he had his own struggles and experiences that were getting in the way of him returning the understanding and effort. Everyone saw it but me. I refused to be honest with myself because I didn't want my investment in "us" to be a waste. I couldn't face the fact that I was loving someone who wasn't able to love me back. I didn't want another failed relationship, so I allowed him to treat me in ways I knew were not acceptable. I was showing up for him but not for me. I couldn't see beyond the blind spots. Showing up requires us to acknowledge the flashing lights—often showing up in the counsel of those who know and love us best—and address them with honesty and vulnerability.

I imagine you are now thinking of times in your life where you haven't shown up. Maybe you're experiencing one of those times right now. To you, I want to say, "It's okay." Consider it an excused absence; your slate is wiped clean. This is a second-chance book and I am a second-chance girl. I got you! You have zero absences starting now. My offer to you is to start showing up from exactly where you are in this present moment. Understand, recognize, and commit to the fact that you are deserving of your own best effort. You are worthy of showing up for yourself and your dreams. Class starts tomorrow morning at 8 AM. Set your alarm and get your plan! I will see you there!

Sharpen Up!

Here are some things you can do to help yourself stay in the present moment:

Breathe. We don't normally think about every breath we take, but being conscious of your breath is a powerful tool. I take four deep breaths when I need to center myself. Sometimes, I will take my index finger and trace a square in order to slow down my breathing. Each line of the square is an inhale or exhale. Draw two squares to get your four breaths in.

Meditate and/or practice yoga. Meditation and yoga have gone mainstream. These ancient practices are good for the body and soul. Sign up for a yoga class in your area or find one online for free. Guided meditation apps are invaluable and will keep you focused if you have trouble keeping your mind from wandering. Even five minutes of solitude goes a long way. The goal is to surrender to the stillness of your mind/thoughts and accept that whatever is happening in this moment is exactly as it is. The next time you are driving, just turn your radio off and drive in the stillness of your thoughts. Where does your mind go? How can you direct it to be still?

Porch sit. Sometimes, I just have to go outside and sit on my porch —without my phone. I use all my senses to note what is happening around me: the sounds of the birds chirping and the cars passing by; the feel of the breeze in my hair; the smell of a passing summer rain. I focus on what I am seeing and hearing in this very moment in order to ground myself where I am right now.

Move! Exercising is an awesome mental reset button. But it doesn't have to be something strenuous, or an activity that requires special gear or clothing. Simply walking at a comfortable pace around your neighborhood will get your body moving and your heart pumping. The act of just moving will help you to find balance and awareness of the present moment.

Limit your screen time. This is a big one for today's world and something I think everyone should consider doing. Put your phone down! Set daily limits for social media or mindless Internet scrolling. Your smart phone will now tell you how much time you are spending scrolling, and it can be shocking. If you have an iPhone, you can actually set a time limit in your settings for downloaded apps. If you aren't sure you have the discipline it takes to stick to your own boundaries, then I recommend doing this for the apps you struggle with. If you have the discipline it takes all on your own—good for you! In that case, create a list of the daily or weekly limits you are setting for yourself and do your best to stick to them. I do my best to only look at my three social media sites twice a day. I find that any more than that starts to affect my mood and motivation.

Instant gratification has not always existed the way it does today. We used to have to wait to get home and receive a phone call or see the blinking light on the answering machine. We can retrain our brains to not be as attached to technology. Pick a time where you are going to "feed" your personal relationships and put your phone in the other room, on silent. This can help you focus on being present and investing in the people right in front of you.

Communicate in the now: Most good conversations are "now" focused. A great communication tool to help tough conversations stay in the present moment is to practice active listening while the other person talks. You are listening to understand, not to plan what you are going to say in response. Look in their eyes or watch their lips and listen. Store the key takeaways in your brain until they are finished talking. When the other person is finished, you respond by saying:

"What I heard you say was… (repeat a summary of what you heard). Is this correct?"

If you are interpreting what the other person is saying correctly, then they will validate this to be the case. An entire conversation can be calmly started and finished by both parties using this listening technique.

The first rule of next chances is simply this: Show up! Go to class. Put one foot in front of the other. You can never make the best grade possible in a class you do not attend. Life is your class. A great life is out there waiting for you, but it requires your attendance. The good news is that no one is excluded from the ability to show up. It isn't dependent on a particular income, relationship status, or level of education. Honesty, effort, and determination are all that is required. Be where your feet are—show up!

CHAPTER 2
You Are Bigger Than Your Fears

"We don't get to choose if we will face frightening
obstacles in life—at some point, we all have to confront
things that scare us—but we do have control over
what power fear has in our lives."

—JAMES CONNER, ARIZONA CARDINALS
RUNNING BACK, FROM HIS BOOK *FEAR IS A CHOICE*

Countless athletes I've worked with over the years have shown up to college with a backpack. Literally. Just a single backpack.

I showed up to college with a U-Haul. I had coordinating bedding, monogrammed with my name on it. I had a refrigerator, microwave, TV, and—since this was 1996, before DVRs and binge-watching were a thing—a VCR, so I could record my can't-miss soap *Days of Our Lives* on a VHS tape every day. I had more clothes than I would ever wear in a semester that I had to pack into a tiny dorm closet, and a backpack full of school supplies that could've carried me to graduation—as if there was no college bookstore or big, chain bargain store nearby that sold these things. With all this apparent enthusiasm, I had no excuse not to succeed; yet I *still* was a mediocre student with a meager drive for success who was terrified of the college classroom.

Fast forward to me being a college counselor. I remember one athlete in particular who had come all the way from the Miami, Florida, area. He rode on a Greyhound bus for over twenty hours to get to Scooba, Mississippi, for his second chance. And he showed up with only a backpack. At the bus station, our coach questioned him: "Dude, where is your stuff?"

"Coach," he replied, "this *is* my stuff. Everything I own is in this backpack—two pairs of clothes and a toothbrush." He had no sheets, no towels, no paper—nothing. Yet he stood there proudly, eager to receive his class schedule and make a name for himself, both on the field and in the classroom.

A different football player wasn't as vocal about what he did and didn't have, but his situation was apparent. The coach who picked him up from a rundown trailer in Mississippi told me the young man's mom handed him a piece of paper with a list on it: toothbrush, toothpaste, deodorant, pencils. She told our coach this was the list of things her son might need at college —things she just couldn't afford to buy.

We never really talked about it, but I knew where he came from and what he was fighting for. He stomped into my office one day, angry as hell, and said, "I quit. I'm leaving. I can't do this."

I stood up, asking forcefully, "And going back to what?"

He thought for a minute. At college, he had a bed, running water, and an all-you-can-eat buffet three times a day. Not to mention a free education. And he wanted to go back to a dead-end existence void of opportunities?

"Ms. Wagner," he finally replied. "I *know* how to do that. I know how to walk my streets and scrap around for my food. I know how to protect myself and how to act in my hometown. I don't know how to do this. I don't know how to walk these halls and act the way y'all want me to act. I don't know how to do any of this. I'm uncomfortable and scared."

These athletes are the reason I can even speak on fear. I had a privileged upbringing; while I've been uncomfortable in my life and struggled with doubts and fears at times, I've seen *real fear* in the eyes of my students. When I finally was wise and mature enough to stop judging and put myself in their shoes, I realized that these men—who were so fierce on the field—were terrified off of it. They were uncomfortable and afraid. Navigating college classrooms and expectations was as scary to them as navigating a football practice would be to me.

Don't Get Trapped in Your Comfort Zone

In life, we naturally gravitate toward places where we are comfortable, fit in, and feel accepted. In fact, psychologist Abraham Maslow's famous five-level Hierarchy of Needs, which theorizes that certain basic needs must be met, in succession, for humans to be motivated to ascend to the next level, lists safety and security as basic needs right alongside water and food. This is often why so many people reenter an abusive relationship after leaving, continue addictive behavior after rehab, or quit an incredible opportunity to go back to what they know. Despite the danger of being abused, they know how to do that. They have adapted and learned how to navigate the chaos that is that situation. Despite the great opportunity of a college football scholarship or the chance to pursue a new relationship, they shrink back because new opportunities can be challenging and uncomfortable. The expectation is too great and the fear of not being enough occupies their minds. And so they return to where they are comfortable; to where they feel they are enough.

These people are not crazy. They are not "less than." They are not fuck-ups. They are allowing fear to control them. Fear is practical and usually explainable. Most of the time, we aren't inventing our fears. The actual feeling of fear is real, it is the story surrounding it that may or may not be true.

I fly often and am not afraid at all. But I have sat beside people on planes who have a huge fear of flying. They take medicine to quell anxiety and react to the slightest bump. In talking to those people, I've noticed they are focused on accounts they've heard about plane crashes. In reality, statistics show you are much more likely to die in a car accident within five miles of your home than to perish in a plane crash. Their fear is real; but it's not based in reality.

I used to be what some would call a Yogi. Merriam-Webster's dictionary defines *yogi* as "a person who practices yoga or an adherent of Yoga philosophy." At the height of my obsession, I practiced yoga as exercise almost every day. I had a group of friends who loved it as much as I did. One woman in our group was turning forty, and for this milestone birthday, her husband generously sent her and ten of her friends on a yoga retreat in Cabo San Lucas, Mexico. I was a broke-as-a-joke, single mom and was completely stoked to be on that top-ten list! We were going to paradise to have five days of yoga with Mandy Ingber, yoga instructor to the stars!

At the time, she was Jennifer Aniston's personal instructor, and I felt I had hit the lottery by getting to soak up her wisdom during that retreat. That trip changed my life—as well as my perception of fear. Mandy Ingber was no joke. This was yoga like I had never experienced it. At home, I practiced yoga about three times a week for an hour at a time. We were practicing twice a day for hours at a time. It was far more intense, mentally and physically, than what I was used to. By day two, my body was already hurting. On day three I was extremely sore and the classes were getting tougher!

I will never forget this moment. I was holding a warrior pose that had me in more of a squat position. Mandy told us that we were going to hold this squat position until our legs were shaking. Then we were going to pulse it out and hold it some more. My legs were shaking and she said, "Pulse!" I thought I was going to collapse as I tried to pulse up and down in the squat. Then she told us to stop pulsing and hold.

Taking a break at the yoga retreat in Cabo San Lucas, Mexico.

What she said next made all the difference. She told us to turn off our brains, to stop thinking about the pain and the feeling in our legs, and just breathe. To sit there in the discomfort rather than give up. To breathe in, relax our minds, and allow our inner strength to take over. I did what she asked. I don't know how much longer I held that squat, but it was for much longer than I thought I could. As we held the squat, she talked about the correlation with our lives. We get uncomfortable and we allow our minds to convince us we aren't strong enough and we can't do it. When we learn to just sit in the discomfort and breathe, we can endure the pain.

When she finally let us release the hold, I cried. I was so much stronger than I was giving myself credit for. I realized it was okay for me to be uncomfortable. I could experience intense pain (emotional pain, too), and I would be okay.

I think we get into a habit of dismissing or numbing our discomforts and fears. We numb the fear of failure, abandonment, and rejection with alcohol, food, and social media. I realized, in my "warrior" moment, to just accept it. To sit in the discomfort, the fear, the pain as it is, rather than dismiss the feelings or try to escape them by quitting. When we face a fear, we need to recognize what we are afraid of and name it. Then we can allow ourselves to be still in that discomfort and hold on, recognizing that it is okay, and we are stronger than we think.

Have you ever known someone who is so afraid of being sick that they are always sick? Or the person who constantly talks about being broke, and when you think about it, they are always broke? Or the person who insists that bad things always happen to them, and—surprise—bad things *do* happen to them? What you focus on expands. I am not discounting true poverty, illness, or hardship. I am not talking about those people who have real, legitimate crises in their lives. No one deserves or creates that. I am talking about the person who doesn't have to experience drama in her life, but because it is what she is always focused on, it exists.

Most of us are guilty of this to some extent. Did you know the physiological makeup of our body is exactly the same when we are anxious or afraid as it is when we are excited or joyful? When I heard this at a conference, the concept blew my mind! But there are countless articles and videos about how these two emotions—that we view as complete opposites—are the same. Both are emotions of arousal.

Both excitement and fear cause our hearts to beat faster and our bodies to release the hormone cortisol. The only difference is our focus. Excitement occurs when we focus on what can go right; anxiety occurs when we focus on what can go wrong. Our bodies are experiencing the same hormonal response, but our minds control the outcome.

Corporations make millions of dollars off our fears. Just the other day, I saw a commercial for a drug to improve bone density. In the commercial, an elderly woman is walking down the stairs. As she is about to step on the next stair, the frame freezes and we see a dog toy that she will slip on, causing her to plummet down the hardwood stairs. The commercial then calls us to ask our doctor about the drug.

Fear! The truth is, no drug is going to prevent an eighty-year-old woman from breaking a bone when she falls down a flight of stairs. But we are afraid of this happening to us or a loved one, so we ask the doctor. I can think of many other examples of how advertising leads us to believe we need certain products to be safe and escape our biggest fears. Our bodies are amazing, but our minds are unbelievably brilliant. I believe we can change our outcome by changing our focus.

There is a scene in season one of *Last Chance U* where I am chasing our star running back, DJ Law, down the hallway of the academic building. As a senior in high school, DJ made headlines when he signed two letters of intent on signing day. One of the most talented running backs coming out of Florida, he accepted scholarship offers from Ole Miss and Utah. The NCAA only allows athletes to pick one school and accept one scholarship. He headlined ESPN as the high-school athlete whose college football dreams were now being based on a time stamp. The NCAA decided whichever offer he faxed in first, based on the time stamp of the fax machine, would be where he would have to attend.

Ultimately, the time stamp didn't matter. DJ would not qualify academically out of high school, and for that reason would end up in Mississippi playing junior college football. He struggled academically, but he struggled more with facing his fears.

The day depicted in *Last Chance U* was no different. DJ was self-sabotaging and I wanted to talk to him about it. I knew I could help him. I knew I had the knowledge and ability to get him out of EMCC and to the next level. I knew we could change his life for the better. But he had to meet me halfway, yet he was running in the opposite direction. Rather than facing his fears, he was trying to escape them.

Once in my office, I gently called him out. "Are you so afraid of failing at all of this that you have resorted to not trying?" I didn't know exactly what he was afraid of. Was he terrified of all the hype being created about his athletic ability? What if he wasn't as talented as everyone thought he was? Or maybe it was an academic fear. Maybe he was afraid that he just wasn't smart enough. And what if he got his hopes up and put all this effort and work behind making the grades and then he fell short of the required 2.5 GPA? That would be the ultimate disappointment.

Instead of finding out, he chose sabotage. Trying and failing was too much to bear. To him, going through the motions with no real effort at all, and simply hoping for the best, seemed like the least scary option. What happened to this athlete? After leaving EMCC, he suffered an injury in

In my office having a serious conversation with DJ Law.

spring practice before his first season of play. Battling academic and personal issues the entire time, he ended up never playing another down of football, not getting his degree, going back where he came from, and ultimately landing himself in jail temporarily.

Whereas if he had put forth the effort, really tried to change his direction in life, if he had gone to class and tutoring, made the grades, and qualified for the scholarship—even if he'd fallen short of his Division I opportunity—he still would have ended up in a better place than where he started.

What realities in your own life are you running from? Where are you failing to put in the effort? It could be a relationship that needs to be mended but the fear of rejection is too great. It could be a desire to go after that dream job, but you worry it won't work out. Or it could be walking into a gym and committing to get healthy, but the fear of not measuring up keeps you away. We all have realities that scare us, insecurities that scream at us. We all have "DJ Law" moments where the fear of trying and failing is so great that we would rather lean on the comfort of knowing we never tried at all.

Effort matters. We may fall short sometimes, but when we push through fear and put forth effort (regardless of whether we believe it will be good enough), we don't fall all the way back to where we started. There is growth, and we shorten our fall. Doing nothing gets us nothing!

Small Steps Add Up to Big Opportunities

Small steps and small successes matter. Every success doesn't have to be a seventy-five-yard run into the end zone. Running backs are among the highest paid positions on the professional football field. They are often considered the most valuable position because of short-yardage bursts. Very rarely do you see a running back break away for 100 yards. Barry Sanders is ranked as one of the best running backs of all time. In 1997, he had over 2,000 rushing yards in eleven games played. That is an average of 125 yards per game. His average rushing yards per attempt? *Six.* He ran for 2,000 yards, six yards at a time. Small successes matter!

This realization has helped me pave the way for athletes who were intimidated by the classroom environment. I would create "small successes" as a way to help them overcome their fears. The first week of classes each semester, English professors would have students write a diagnostic essay. The essays weren't graded; the professors just wanted a sample to assess their students' abilities and deficiencies. Because the pressure of failing was removed, the guys who were afraid of writing could relax and just write. I would then ask the professors to grade the papers of the athletes and return to me the A's and the B's.

Without fail, that stack would include papers from some of the very football players who didn't believe they were smart enough to be in college. I would call each of them into my office individually and go berserk over the "A" they had just made on their first college essay. I would make it a celebration and a massive accomplishment. In reality, the grade wasn't even going in the grade book. But it wasn't about the grade. That moment of creating and celebrating a small success gave these guys the confidence and momentum to move forward and tackle the semester in the same way they would the opposing team—with all their might and force. It gave them the motivation to put forth effort and the belief that they could make a good grade in that class. By allowing yourself to celebrate even your smallest milestones, you set yourself up for success in the future.

This requires baby steps. Practice. Patience. And work. One successful moment probably isn't going to flip the switch and create a world of sunshine and rainbows. But it can create a victory, one small moment at a time. Not backing down in the face of our fear is a choice that we sometimes have to make every single day, sometimes multiple times a day.

The X's and O's of Fear

Let's break this down with a little more detail, talking through a common fear—the fear of failure. This is a fear I am well-acquainted with. This fear is complex and deeply rooted.

When I work with an athlete plagued with the "fear of failure," we begin by naming it and owning it rather than dismissing it. Look inward and ask the following questions:

- What am I trying *not* to fail at?
- What does failure look like in this scenario?
- How am I defining success in this scenario?
- What would cause success instead of failure?
- Am I doing anything to sabotage my own success in this area?

Think through these questions and talk about them out loud (even if only to yourself), then get out a piece of paper and write down your answers.

The next step is to make a plan. What needs to happen for this attempt to be successful? For the athlete sabotaging his academic success, his first step was to go to class. To accomplish that, he needed a sustainable plan for getting up each morning and getting to class on time. He needed to walk in the door, which required a plan for self-discipline surrounding his sleep habits and attitude. He needed to learn his teachers' names for added accountability, and to practice body language that mimicked someone who was paying attention. He would eventually need to take notes or record the information he would need to be successful on graded assignments. This might mean taking the notes himself or asking someone for help.

You can see where this exercise is going. Take your fear and do the same. Figure out what needs to happen around your attempt in order to make your attempt successful and then develop a plan to do those things. Remember that it's about the small victories, such as setting your alarm for an hour earlier so you can get up and exercise, or filling out the job application and turning it in. You don't have to go from the fear of water to swimming in the ocean. Start small with actionable details and work your way up. Celebrate each small success and take one day at a time. All the while, keep your focus and thoughts on what can go *right*!

You must be brave and vulnerable when facing a fear. You also have to show up and do the hard work. You've picked up this book, so you are clearly on the path to creating something different for yourself and committing to making a change in your life. Let's briefly talk about the role of other people in this journey. There will be people who support you on your new journey and there will always be critics who doubt you. Let me say this: The critic is not the one who counts! In my opinion, those who aren't able to support new journeys and positive transitions are suffering from their own insecurities and jealousy. You do not need these people's feedback! Remain focused on your own goals and the inner circle of people who will support you and help you to get there. People sitting on their couches, not doing the hard work, do not get to comment on your efforts or attempts. People who know little of what you're battling through do not get a say. As Theodore Roosevelt stated in his 1910 "The Man in the Arena" Speech:

It is not the critic who counts; not the man who points out how the strong man stumbles, or where the doer of deeds could have done them better. The credit belongs to the man who is actually in the arena, whose face is marred by dust and sweat and blood; who strives valiantly; who errs, who comes up short again and again, because there is no effort without error and shortcoming; but who does actually strive to do the deeds; who knows great enthusiasms, the great devotions; who spends himself in a worthy cause; who at the best knows in the end the triumph of high achievement, and who at the worst, if he fails, at least fails while daring greatly, so that his place shall never be with those cold and timid souls who neither know victory nor defeat.

To put that in plain English, you are the strong one and you are in your own ring putting forth effort to become a better version of yourself. You are a product of your own experiences and only you know exactly how those experiences look and feel. I hope that a close-knit inner circle of people stand in the ring with you. They may be helping you to fight the actual battle. They sweat and bleed and cry with you, and when you are face-down in that ring after getting your ass kicked, so are they. If you do not think you have a support system, I am going to challenge you to open your eyes a little wider and extend your gaze a little further, because you do. Your cheerleaders may not be blood relatives, close friends, or the coworker in the next cubicle. That's okay. Find the positive people who exist in your life, wherever they may be. It could be a teacher, a neighbor, an acquaintance at the gym. Sometimes cheerleaders are individuals we have never met. I have many "fans" who cheer me on constantly and are encouraging members of my team. I have never met them in person, but they are in the ring with me.

Do you remember being afraid of the dark as a child? The darkness, or fear of it, didn't just go away—no matter how fearful we were, we had to be in the dark at times. As children, our parents or guardians held our hand in the dark room or they looked under the bed to assure us nothing sinister lurked beneath. They plugged in night-lights or lie beside us on a particularly frightening night until we fell asleep. As adults, we can reach out to the supportive people in our lives who will help us face our fears. Fears are not nearly as scary when we don't have to face them alone.

Going back to the idea of battling in the ring, when you find yourself face-down, look around from that angle and see who is at eye level. Who is holding your hand? Who is sitting on the outside, looking down at you? Those who do not have the courage to step in the arena do not get to pass judgment on how you are fighting your fight. When you put forth effort and do something hard, there will be times where you stumble and fall. But you will fall fighting for a worthy cause—YOUR LIFE! You are greater, stronger, and braver than your biggest fear! I believe it, and to overcome your fears, you need to believe it, too.

Sharpen Up!

Name the fear. Don't hide or make excuses for what is holding you back. Naming the fear and calling it out brings it into the light. Secrets have power. When we bring secrets into the light, we minimize the power they hold over us.

Shift the focus. Fear is a choice. We can call it out, but then we need to shift our focus to overcoming it. I do this with vision boards, visualizations, and positive mantras.

- **Vision boards.** I make at least one vision board a year. Using a poster board and magazines, I tear out pictures that speak to me or inspire me. Don't overthink this the first time through, just start tearing. I wait a few days and go back through the pictures I tore out and think about what they mean to me and which ones are still inspiring to me. Next I use a glue stick and let creativity go wild as I arrange the pictures on the poster board. I use markers to write in any words, quotes, or ideas I want to be central for my year. When I'm finished, I hang the vision board in a place where I will at least glance at it once a day. I have three hanging right now in my closet!

- **Visualizations.** Close your eyes and regularly visualize yourself doing the thing you are trying to accomplish. Do this daily or several times a day. There is no magic number as to how often you might need to stop and visualize. Be aware of your mental state. When you find yourself in a moment of self-doubt or worry, stop, and visualize your success. I have known athletes who visualize their game performance before every game. They mentally take themselves through the warm-up, the execution of certain plays, and even winning the game. They visualize themselves performing successfully from beginning to end. When you are visualizing yourself as successful in scary situations, you are focused on what can go right—not your fear!

- **Mantras.** My favorite therapist told me to start reciting mantras. He wrote one out on a card for me to start with: *"Light surrounds me; power protects me; love envelops me; presence watches over me; wherever I am, God is."* I memorized this and also hung it on my office bulletin board. I still find myself repeating it at times when I feel alone and helpless. Find quotes, Bible verses, or simple empowering phrases such as, "I am enough," "I am loved," or "Fear is a choice" and stick them to the mirrors in your house or the dashboard of your car. Here's a saying I like to keep in mind: Say it, see it, believe it, and become it!

Make a plan and put in effort. Wanting to do something and creating a *plan* to do it are two different things. If I wanted to drive cross-country from Birmingham to Los Angeles, I wouldn't just hop in my car this afternoon and take off. I would look at different routes I could take and map out the one I was the most excited about. Before leaving, I would take my car in for a tune-up. I would make sure my house was secure, and that I'd covered my parental responsibilities. I would pack and set a date and time to leave. A plan ensures that the trip is enjoyable and goes smoothly.

The plan also motivates me to actually make the trip. I can dream of driving cross-country daily, but what are the chances of me actually going for it if I never plan it out? Same goes for overcoming our fears. We are more likely to go for it if we plan for it!

Celebrate small successes. Give yourself benchmarks and reasons to celebrate. You completed all graded assignments for the week in your first week of going back to school. You shared for the first time in the support group you are attending. You walked into a gym and asked a personal trainer to help you with formulating a workout plan. Though simple to achieve, each of these actions is a success. Big victories come from small, daily successes. Celebrations can be as simple as a high five or phoning a friend. They may also increase over time to indulging in a nice dinner or purchasing a new outfit. You choose! Just make sure to stop long enough to celebrate your achievements!

Form your team. Who is in your ring? Identify the people in your life who you trust and who are rooting for you. This support system—or inner circle—can encourage and motivate you, but they can also be honest and hold you accountable to what you are trying to achieve. Cheerleaders are fine sometimes—but we also need coaches.

The athletes I work with often show up with few material belongings. But they carry lots of emotional baggage: fears that have been reinforced throughout their lives. Fears of failure or of not being enough. Fears of injury that will make them look "weak" or derail their athletic career. Fears of only being an athlete and achieving nothing more in life. Part of my job has been to show them how to identify those fears and change their thinking so they can shift their focus. The instructions are usually simple. The hard part is choosing to take the steps necessary to gain forward momentum. To do something different. The hard part is recognizing and believing that you are worth it! You are bigger than your fears! Choose freedom over fear and break free of the control fear possesses in your life. You can do it!

CHAPTER 3
Be Prepared for Your Success

"We are only in control of two things:
how we prepare for what might happen and how we
respond to what just happened. The moment when
things actually do happen belongs to God."
—DEVON FRANKLIN

I filmed two seasons of *Last Chance U*. I enjoyed every minute of filming season one. Season two, however, while still an amazing experience, was much more stressful to film. During that season, I faced increasing outside pressure as well as my own internal battle. The show was huge—millions of people had seen it and now knew who I was. It seemed like they all wanted to talk to me, see me, and hear what I had to say. People were traveling to campus from all over the country (and even from abroad) and often showed up unannounced in my office. I was constantly asked for pictures or just stared at, which I'll admit was disconcerting. On the flip side, my platform had suddenly exploded into something bigger than I could have imagined.

Internally, I wrestled with what to do with my newfound influence. Questions swirled in my mind. *Should I just sit back and enjoy being the sweetheart of college football while it lasts? After eight years, should I stay firmly planted, working with the athletes at East Mississippi Community College? Should I go on raising my daughter in our small Mississippi town? Or should I use this exciting, new platform as a springboard to do something bigger?* My success on *Last Chance U* seemed like my shot to impact more people, be my own boss, and take control of my life and work. I could go wherever I wanted to go. *Should I leave the school and go out on my own?* I wondered.

I had felt the itch to do something more start to creep in the year before we actually started filming *Last Chance U*. I wanted to advance in my career. I had learned a tremendous amount during my time working with various types of student athletes, and I felt I was ready to instruct and lead other young counselors. Unfortunately, EMCC was not where that would happen.

I had started to apply for positions at larger, four-year universities. I interviewed with several powerhouse programs—LSU, UNC, University of Tennessee, and Ole Miss. Some rejected me, and some I rejected. (Thank goodness for rejection because it allowed me to be featured in a Netflix documentary.) Once we began filming, I committed to doing my best work. I realized I *was* actually accomplishing my dream of "leading young counselors" through my influence on the show. But when we began filming season two, none of it felt right anymore. I faced an internal struggle of living out my now-famous season one line: "God, put me where I am most effective. Put me where I can impact the most people." I was lying to myself: Scooba, Mississippi, was no longer my platform—I longed to spread my wings.

But walking away from my full-time job as an athletic academic counselor at EMCC meant walking away from the security of a steady paycheck, health insurance, and a retirement fund. While I'm sure many people imagine I was compensated generously for my work on *Last Chance U*, I didn't receive a dime. As a matter of policy, Netflix does not pay subjects of a documentary series, believing that money will alter the reality of the documentary. Not only did I not get paid to film the show, I also received no compensation for the promotion of it.

I was a single mom. My daughter was counting on me. I didn't have the steady income of a husband to rely on if things didn't work out, or a million dollars in the bank. I wrestled with my options and thought about them constantly. *Would going out on my own be irresponsible? Was I "good enough" to make it work? What would I do if my plan failed miserably?*

I realized I needed to set aside my emotions and begin to prepare and plan for what was next. I sifted through the thousands of e-mails and social media messages I had received and replied to those asking if I did public speaking or consulting. I reached out to colleagues and contacts who had knowledge about details, such as how much to charge, how to create a contract, and what to talk about from the stage. I kept my full-time position but began speaking on the side to feel it out as a career move. I created my own website so fans and potential clients could contact me. A step at a time, I began preparing myself to be an independent consultant and motivational speaker.

Months later, I was in a coffeehouse in Birmingham, Alabama, when two men approached me and told me they were fans of *Last Chance U*. They asked me what I was doing with my newfound fame. I quipped something about trying to just keep my head above water.

One of them asked me what I wanted to do.

The words poured right out. "I want to use my platform to help as many people as I can while being my own boss."

"Well, do it!" he said.

I sat in that coffee shop for hours that day with these two men. No doubt something bigger than me brought them to me. One was a small business consultant and the other a marketing, branding, and technology guru.

I drove back to Meridian, Mississippi, and sat on my bedroom floor with a notebook and a pencil. In the first column, I wrote down every essential expense. I figured out exactly how much it would cost for Kennedy and me to live comfortably. In the second column, I wrote down every speaking engagement I had booked and how much each was paying. I did the math and figured out I could pay my bills for six months off the speaking gigs alone. During those six months, I would have to figure out how to capitalize and make the job—that is, working for myself—work long-term.

Months later, I walked into the college president's office and told him my last day at EMCC would be February 14, 2017. I was scared to death. I knew this decision would affect a lot of people I cared about. The athletes at EMCC would be devastated and worried about their futures. The film crew and producer would have to figure out how to make *Last Chance U* without me. My daughter and the lives of my family would be impacted tremendously. The fans of the show would be disappointed. But I had spent time planning for this change, and I trusted I was making the right decision.

My social media post on February 6 read:

This has been a very tough decision to make, but I have decided to leave

East Mississippi Community College to pursue another career opportunity. I will forever be better for having worked with the student-athletes of
EMCC. I am beyond grateful for that opportunity. I consistently ask athletes to let go of the fears in life and go for it. Now I am reminding myself
to do the same. Kennedy and I are so excited for our new adventures. And
yes, we have our pencils!

Don't Fall into the Trap of Paralysis by Analysis

I had prepared, but I didn't have every single detail mapped
out before I made the leap. There is a fine line between planning and
overplanning—or obsessing. Overplanning can cause us to freeze
because we never feel ready to start. Fear may tell us we must achieve
perfection before we can go after something.

We have to have all our debt paid off or a house with a white-picket
fence before we can have a baby. We have to know 100 percent that
every single one of our preferences will be met before we take the leap
into a new job. We feel we must possess the perfect website, logo, and
full funding before we start a new company. And when things don't
fall exactly into place, we wait, and wait, and wait...because it never
seems like the perfect time, the perfect person, or the perfect opportunity. Preparation does not mean perfection.

In all preparation, there is a component of "Fake it 'til you make it."
No matter how well I prepare, I have never had it all figured out. In
motherhood, in my career, in life—most of the time I feel like I have
no idea what I am doing. In fact, most people don't! Part of preparation is just figuring out how to keep moving forward and acting on
what is known while faking what is not. This has been the theme of
my entire life.

From my perspective, the key to my success has been risk-taking. I do my research and prepare as well as I can, then I go for it, whether I feel ready or not! Are there opportunities I could have capitalized on more if I'd been better prepared? Maybe. But would I have had as *many* opportunities and experiences if I'd waited until I felt ready? Probably not. My exact level of preparation, along with my exact moments of faking it, have brought me to the exact place I am supposed to be.

Sometimes you just have to leap. None of us has it all figured out. No one has all the answers. In fact, when we elevate people to superhuman status, we usually end up disappointed when we learn they are actually just human. Remember a few years ago when celebrities started being brutally honest about what they really looked like? It was devastating and reassuring all at the same time. Turns out *People* magazine's "Most Beautiful Person" was manufactured and nobody wakes up like that—not even Beyoncé.

Step Bravely into the Future

I think all of us have a fraction of that "not good enough" fear. Social media has exacerbated this as it tempts us to compare ourselves to others—and comparison is the thief of joy. The bravest thing to do is to own our fear. Instead of being ashamed of the strength of our stories and our own truths, we need to understand that the things we don't know make us human as much as the things we do know. *Imposter syndrome* is feelings of inadequacy that persist even when success is evident. Most of us have probably felt this way at some point during our lives. Maya Angelou, one of the greatest writers and most influential women of all time, once admitted: "I have run game on everybody, and they're going to find me out." I believe we are all running game. The only thing that will be "found out" about us is that we are human. We are not imposters—we are human beings.

Athletes are no different. Sometimes we elevate them to a "super-human" status in our minds, but it turns out they are just ordinary human beings. The physical and mental preparation needed to be one of these humans is intense. The average fan likely knows little about the grueling preparation athletes go through. An athlete's life is full of weight workouts, conditioning runs, position practices, team practices, position meetings, team meetings, film review, game run-throughs, and more!

I saw this firsthand when I visited an NFL training facility. I have become a Dallas Cowboys fan in recent years. Dak Prescott, the Cowboys quarterback, played at my alma mater in Mississippi, and I've had the privilege of meeting him a few times. So when the Cowboys drafted him, they gained a fan in me. Several years ago, I was speaking in Dallas and received an invite to tour not only AT&T Stadium where the Cowboys play on Sunday, but also the Star, the practice facility where the team and staff spend Monday through Saturday. I did my best to contain my excitement, but I'm pretty sure I took a hundred pictures.

I was amazed at the resources and energy spent on preparation alone. Forget the games. By the time these players play in an actual game, there is nothing more they can do. They have spent an entire week (or longer) preparing. There were rooms for everything—every aspect had been planned. The weight room had a protein shake bar where each player received his customized protein shake after working out. The cafeteria had specific meal plans for each player, designed to nourish his body for maximum performance. A portion of the roof was a turf field. When I asked my tour guide about it, he explained that the defensive team meeting rooms were on the second floor.

Sometimes the players would be going over plays on paper and need to actually "act out" the play or scenario. To accommodate this need, they turned the roof into a mini field.

Preparation leads to less stress and paves the way for success. Teams and players who feel prepared have more fun on game day. They play with an unshakeable type of confidence. Preparation is a dress rehearsal for success. It inspires the confidence we need to break through fear and go after our goals. It sends a signal to ourselves and those around us that says, "I am ready and eager for my next venture. I believe I will be successful."

Successful Opportunities Require Resources

In my twenties, I worked at a university that competed in the Southeastern Conference (SEC), which I view as the best college athletics conference in the country. I started out as the lowest level of academic counselor on staff, and then earned a promotion. I was now in charge of study hall/tutoring services, and the boss of hundreds of tutors, four graduate assistants, and one full-time employee, Mrs. Shelly. Mrs. Shelly was older than me. She ran our study hall and tutoring services at night for our athletes. In my position, I oversaw all our student success services, and therefore I was responsible for study hall, tutoring, and Mrs. Shelly.

Mrs. Shelly loved her job and she loved our student-athletes. She would have done anything to help each one of them succeed. She had an entire plastic bin full of pens, pencils, and highlighters, and she would hand them out like candy to the athletes who needed them. "Book scholarship" athletes were given their textbooks and calculators and they could also rent laptops from us. At the time, other supplies were not included in what we could buy them. "Non-book

At Dak Prescott's locker in the Dallas Cowboys locker room.

scholarship" athletes were not allowed even textbooks to be furnished. They had to purchase all their academic supplies. Thus, I showed up to work one morning and got called into my boss's office. I was told that Mrs. Shelly had been handing out pencils to athletes and that could get us in trouble. Providing improper benefits to athletes was an NCAA infraction, and my boss felt this could be viewed as such. He instructed me to reprimand her and put a stop to this.

I was young and trying to impress my boss and everyone else, so I didn't bat an eye. When she reported to work that day, I called her into my office. I reprimanded her, explaining this could get us in "big trouble." She complied with no argument. Looking back, however, I am willing to bet she wanted to slap some sense into me. She knew my heart. And she knew I was aware that she had been handing out resources to help our athletes for some time. We both knew there was absolutely nothing wrong with this and could not give two shits if the NCAA agreed or not. Nonetheless, we stopped handing out pencils to athletes that day. So it's funny that I'm now famous for the very same thing that got Mrs. Shelly into trouble: handing out pencils to athletes. My famous line on *Last Chance U*, "Do you have a pencil?" is what has endeared many viewers to me.

Mrs. Shelly died suddenly not long after I had made the transition to EMCC. I took off work to make the drive and attend her funeral. I was shocked and sad. As I sat there coming to terms with the fact that she was gone, I was upset (and worried) for the athletes whom she loved. Who was going to help them? How would they respond when she wasn't there every night? I got mad at myself for not supporting her more, for telling her to stop handing out pencils. The more I thought about it, the angrier I became—at everyone. How could my boss care so little about the success of our students? How could the NCAA say that pencils were an improper benefit when they were a key resource to being prepared and successful in class? They sure didn't consider resources on the field, such as cleats and pads, as an improper benefit.

That was the day I stopped at the Dollar General and bought ten packs of pencils and put them in a red tin can on my desk. If I was going to sell an opportunity, ask athletes to show up, demand effort, I would be damned if I denied them the right to a key ingredient to their preparation and academic success. *Need a pencil? Here, have one. Have two!*

The reason I hand out pencils like candy is because preparation is key to success. And resources are a part of preparation. To give someone an opportunity but not provide the resources necessary for him or her to be successful is not an opportunity. Here's what I mean: We provide college scholarships to athletes that require them to maintain a certain academic standard. But we won't give them the basic supplies they need to accomplish the goal. Resources are an essential part of preparation. The two go hand in hand to create a recipe for success.

Do you need a pencil? Fans around the world mailed me over 4,000 pencils after the first season of the show aired.

This is a book about second chances—and third and fourth ones, too. Just like we need resources in order to maximize our success, we also need change. No matter what your next chance looks like—a career change, a divorce, or a habit change—we have to leave something behind to succeed in a new opportunity. Most people never take the time to process why the first chance did not work out or why they outgrew that situation and needed another challenge. They don't pause to contemplate how they must prepare to make this new opportunity different. If we go into our second chance with the same mindset, attitude, and actions that sunk our first attempt, we can expect the same outcome. There are, of course, external factors that contribute to the success and failure of one's efforts; however, if we experience multiple failures or botched relationships, we must at least consider that *we* may be the common denominator. The faster we decide to change our attitude, mindset, and preparation methods, the sooner we will see progress.

Sharpen Up!

What is the WHY? We need to do something different to make our second chances different from their predecessors. The question we must ask ourselves is *WHY*? Why are we feeling the push to create change and for what purpose? Let's be very clear with ourselves before plunging into something new. Take the time to define exactly what you want to do and why. Here are some examples of how to write this in mission statement form:

- *(What) I will break the cycle of allowing toxic people in my life, (Why) so I can model better relationships to my children.*

- *(What) I will finish my education, (Why) so I can create a better life for myself that includes moving out of my hometown.*

This is your opportunity to dream. Put thought into exactly what it is you are looking to change and be specific about *why* you are fired up to get it done!

Put pencil to paper. A good plan contains details. If you don't have the discipline to put together a specific plan, you probably don't have the discipline to follow through on an opportunity. Let's use the example of losing weight:

> "I am going to lose weight," says the person who wants to lose weight.

> "That's great. How?" says the supportive friend who has heard this before.

> "I'm going to eat less."

As well-meaning as that person may be, if he or she were disciplined enough to just eat less, there wouldn't be a billion-dollar weight-loss industry. We break habits using specific action plans. This is the "how" part of preparation. *How* are you going to accomplish your goal?

Examples of specific action steps:

- I am going to keep a food diary for a week to see exactly what I am eating, when, and how much.

- I am going to go to counseling once a week for six months, and work through my own issues so I can be more like the person I want to attract.

- I am going to participate in a five-day juice cleanse and then re-introduce certain foods slowly back into my diet.

- I am going to attend study hall/tutoring four times a week to improve my grades.

Pull together your resources. Make a list of the resources you need to be successful. For example, a website advertising your new business, a suit to wear to your next job interview, a tutor to help you bring up your grade. Remember, these resources don't have to get you to the end result. An athlete's end goal may be to play for a Power Five program, but right now he or she needs to earn a B in this chemistry class to maintain eligibility. What resources do you need *right now* to take advantage of a new opportunity? I created my own website on Squarespace because I knew a website was a resource I needed for my new business of speaking and consulting. I didn't pay a ton of money for the site, and it wasn't fancy, but it allowed fans and potential clients to find me. As my business grew, I slowly upgraded my website and eventually hired someone to run it for me. But I didn't start out that way. Don't feel like you have to "go big or go home." Start small and allow yourself to grow over time.

Decide on your nonnegotiables. In order to avoid over-planning, write down the five must-haves for pulling the trigger on an opportunity. My biggest nonnegotiable was having the ability to pay my bills for six months. Without that security, I felt it was unwise to move forward and quit my job. Here are a few other examples of nonnegotiables:

- A working website

- $10,000 in savings

- Six months of being alone

- One year of sobriety

- Finding enough scholarships to pay for 40 percent of tuition and fees for college

The beauty of listing nonnegotiables, or the essentials, is we give ourselves a free pass on the negotiables. Do not push pause on your dream or give up because of picky excuses or details that aren't on the list. That is fear talking! Stick to your essentials and when those are met, go for it!

Take hints from others. Chances are there is someone already doing what you want to do and doing it well. That is okay! There is enough room at the table for everyone. We don't have to take one another out or view ourselves or the competition as the winner or loser. We can all be successful. There is enough for everyone! There are actually thousands of absolutely amazing athletic academic counselors. I just happened to be the one on a Netflix show. That doesn't mean I am any better than any of the others, or that my methods are the best. We can all be successful in our own space and with our own philosophies. Learn from others—both what *to* do and what *not* to do! These people can be coworkers, neighbors, friends, family members, or even strangers; we can literally learn from anyone. What do you like and dislike about what they are doing? What is working and not working, and how would you do it differently? You can find value in what is already being done and build on it.

Why did I walk the hallways of East Mississippi Community College and hand out pencils to some of the top athletes in the country? Because they didn't have one. Manifesting success without the necessary resources is extremely hard. If you want to pass a class, you need to have a pencil. If you want to start a business, you need to have a plan. It's that simple, but we tend to complicate that plan and make excuses for why we "can't" succeed. Success hinges on proper planning, which prepares us for the big things we know are coming. Set yourself up for success and make the leap! Your opportunity is coming!

CHAPTER 4
When Opportunity Knocks

"What is important is that you make the leap.
Jump high and hard with intention and heart."
—CHERYL STRAYED

I f I've heard it once, I've heard it a hundred times. "I *just* want an opportunity to play at the next level." I've heard a version of this from every junior college athlete I've ever worked with. The offer comes—but it's Akron University offering a scholarship, not *the* Ohio State University. "I am not playing *there*. I'm a better player than that. I deserve a better offer." We all *just* want an opportunity—until it is not the opportunity we want.

Wyatt Roberts was the starting quarterback at EMCC during the filming of the first season of *Last Chance U*. He was an extremely good football player and also focused on his academics. He was also just a good ol' country boy. He was the sixth All-American quarterback in a row that EMCC had produced. Three of the five before him continued on to play in the Southeastern Conference (SEC). His backup QB was John Franklin III, a transfer from Florida State. Although John was an exceptional athlete, Wyatt fought for the position and won the coveted starting spot fair and square and proved himself on the field.

Catching up with former EMCC quarterbacks John Franklin III and Wyatt Roberts at an Auburn University football game.

At the end of the season when scholarship offers starting trickling in, Wyatt wanted to continue his football career and was hopeful he'd earned a Division I offer. He hadn't. He received a Division III offer to play at Mississippi College (MC). His backup, John Franklin, was headed to Auburn after one spectacular showing. As fate would have it, the Auburn scout was at that game. In a conversation, aired on the show, Wyatt expressed his frustration in MC being his only offer. He said he would turn it down and quit playing football. He wasn't going DIII when the three guys before him—and his backup QB—got SEC opportunities. Wyatt *wanted* to play, but he didn't *need* to play. He only wanted to continue his career if he could play at the highest level. He knew exactly what he wanted.

Breaking Down Your Dream

Before we evaluate if the opportunity sitting in front of us is "right" or "wrong," we need to actually define what we want. If your goal is to "play college football," break down that goal into specifics. Define what "play" means to you. Here are a few examples:

- I want to be a top player on the team and in the starting lineup with maximum playing time.

- I want to be on the field but don't want the pressure. I'm okay backing up athletes with more experience or talent.

- I want to earn a scholarship to be a part of the team as a practice player, which I understand means sitting the bench during games.

- I want to walk on with no scholarship and participate in a minimal way as a player. I just want to be a part of a team.

All of these goals are technically "an opportunity to play at the next level," but each one is different in its details. Write down your actual desire and spell out the details. This process may take time and require honest self-evaluation to determine the actual desire. There might be more than one way to narrow down the goal or dream. Be as specific as possible. Identifying a good opportunity is difficult when our goal is vague.

Za'Darius Smith has played in the NFL as a defensive lineman for five years. Before he was in the NFL, he only had a few years of football experience. He was a basketball player at Greenville High School in Greenville, Alabama, when the football coach approached him his junior year. The coach asked him to try out for the football team. Z is six-foot-four and 272 pounds. I feel like he came into the world that size, but I am sure he was a little bit smaller in high school. He started playing football that year and decided to stick with it. He had one

Visiting with Za'Darius Smith.

scholarship offer out of high school. One. A football scholarship meant a free ride to a college education. The offer was to play football at this tiny little junior college in equally tiny Scooba, Mississippi: East Mississippi Community College. Our defensive coordinator told me about this new player I would soon meet. He told me about the young man's raw talent, despite his lack of experience. If Za'Darius capitalized on his opportunity, the coordinator told me, he would play in the NFL one day.

I found that hard to believe. Za'Darius had a long way to go. But after his second season playing junior college football, he had just about every big-time program in the country offering him a scholarship—a whopping eighty-two offers! (Most athletes receive five to ten!) He was overwhelmed by the possibilities and had no idea how to make the decision. I created a chart with a pencil and a piece of paper to help him make one of the most important decisions of his life. I ended up using that same chart on many athletes who came after him.

"What are the top five things you want in your college football experience?" I asked as we sat down to fill out the chart. "Be specific about what it is you want, Za'Darius. Your success and happiness depend on it." I gave him some examples: "Do you want to be close to home? Do you want large crowds? Swag?" He wrote down his top five must-haves. From the offers before him, we eliminated all that were a hard no based on his criteria. We continued to narrow down the list until five schools remained. He could take five official visits—all expenses paid—to check out his top five choices in person.

Recruiting trips are amazing. The athletes eat steak for every meal and walk onto the field with their pictures on the Jumbotron and crowd noise piped in over the loudspeaker. Everything is perfect—a perfect lie. This is the only time these athletes will be treated like this. If the athletes are vulnerable to being swept off their feet, the schools with the most resources win every time. But time and time again, I have observed that decisions based on smoke and mirrors or an ego trip can lead to disappointment and unhappiness with the outcome.

When we get caught up in the hoopla (either about ourselves or the opportunity), we make the decision based on how we feel in the moment rather than what we actually want. Marketers, job recruiters, and football coaches are experts at manipulating our desires so they can benefit. This is how we get sucked into forgetting the entire reason we wanted the opportunity in the first place. We lose when we get caught up in the moment; we win when we know exactly what we want.

Z used the chart to focus on what was important to him. When the big-money schools attempted to dazzle and entice him, he was able to ignore it. He focused on his five deal breakers and his five must-haves. He turned down four powerhouse football programs to play at the University of Kentucky, a basketball powerhouse. Tons of college football fans thought he was crazy. However, over the next two years, he became the face of Kentucky football. He contributed immediately, became the dominant figure on the defense, and thrived in all areas of his life. He also helped turn UK football into a next-level competitor. Most importantly, he graduated. I still have his graduation invitation framed on a bookshelf in my office. He made a smart, informed decision and picked the best opportunity for him—not the shiniest or the most popular. In 2015, the Baltimore Ravens drafted Za'Darius in the fourth round of the NFL draft. In 2019, he signed a four-year, $66 million contract with the Green Bay Packers.

All That Glitters Is Not Gold—Stay Focused

We can follow Z's example by staying focused on what we want. The athletes I work with use my "recruiting chart." They stay focused on the five criteria listed on the top row of that chart in order to make the best decision. Make your own opportunity chart. What are the five essential qualities you are looking for in this next opportunity? List each quality along the top row and each of your opportunities down the left-hand column. Now decide which opportunity provides you the best chance at satisfying your essential qualities. Circle the opportunity that "wins" each of the five categories. Whichever opportunity is circled the most is more than likely the right one for you.

If "immediate contribution" is in your top five, do research to answer the questions, "Where will I fit in?" and "How many people are ahead of me on the 'depth chart'?" If there are already fifteen other defensive linemen on the team with more experience and bigger builds, then don't get swept away by the "picture on the Jumbotron" moment. Chances are yours will never be there. And you will be standing on the sideline miserable, watching all the other linemen run through the tunnel wishing you had just chosen…Akron.

Maybe you have a detailed goal but no actual opportunities have presented themselves. That's okay. It's highly possible they just haven't presented themselves *yet*. While you wait, put those specific desires out into the universe—speak them, affirm them, see them, ask for them. You don't have to do this in an overly confident, arrogant way. Many who have believed a dream into existence possess a quiet, subtle confidence. What we believe, we become. We have a way of manifesting our true desires when we are humble enough to ask for them.

Opportunities are out there. Sometimes we just get distracted by the shiny ones. We turn down more opportunities in life than we capitalize on because they aren't "good enough," we are not willing to do the work, or we are afraid. Not all great opportunities are shiny. As a matter of fact, I believe we often encounter marvelous opportunities wrapped in dust rather than diamonds: ones that test our work ethic and our intentions. We must be open to recognizing our chances. Remember Chapter 1? We will not see the chances that are sitting right in front of us if we are not showing up. Once we ask for the opportunity, we must open our eyes, ears, and hearts to identifying it when it arrives—even if it is not as spectacular as we had hoped.

Keep It Real

Some opportunities are disappointing, but they are *still* opportunities. It's normal to be disappointed and emotional when expectations are not met or opportunities don't pan out. But the response that follows is key. This is where we are prone to get it wrong and dismiss or destroy a chance to grow.

When opportunities don't look the way you hoped they would, allow yourself to feel what you feel. For example, maybe you were expecting a job with a six-figure salary and the salary is a fraction of that. You can be angry, anxious, confused, upset, disappointed, or sad. Allow the emotion but give yourself a deadline. For me, the deadline is usually twenty-four hours. Any more time than that and I sink into a long-term pity party. I struggle to crawl out of the negativity and get back into my logical brain if I sit in my emotions for too long. After my deadline is up, I have to get real with myself. Go back to your original questions.

Why did I want this in the first place?

What is the end goal?

Is this a punch to my ego and is that why I'm upset? Or is it actually the wrong fit for me?

Taking it back to the "Why?" helps ground us in logic, rather than emotion. Don't get me wrong; emotions are real. The story we make up surrounding them is usually not. Get real with yourself and your ego about the opportunity in front of you. Our egos can get in our way and tell us we deserve something better. I don't know about you, but quite frankly, I don't want what I deserve. I am human, and although I am committed to grow and evolve as a person, I fall short of perfection ALL of my days. In the moments where I fall short, getting "what I deserve," what I might think I am somehow owed, would actually be far less than the blessings I currently possess if I only took the time to notice. I want to be mindful of and grateful for the blessings I already have. Our attitudes surrounding our next chance will make or break us. If we are focused on negativity, we will create a negative outcome. If we are grateful and express our gratitude that we indeed have an opportunity, we can be proud of the outcome we create.

Our Toughest Opponent May Be the One in the Mirror

Everything is falling into place for our second chance, then we self-sabotage. Sometimes, our feelings get in our way. We let our unconscious fear win. I think we do this the most in relationships, but it can certainly happen in other areas as well. Relationships are subjective, so pinpointing the exact problem can be difficult. We tend to project past fears onto people who did not create them. For example, my ex-husband cheated on me. This was painful and traumatizing. I know I have deep-rooted fears (and triggers) around infidelity. In every relationship since my divorce, I have projected those fears onto the new man, which only creates distrust and more pain.

For years I didn't see that my own unconscious fears and trust issues were contributing to these men either running or cheating. I subconsciously chose the kind of men who were apt to do these things —what I focused on became a self-fulfilling prophecy of betrayal and abandonment. Through therapy and hard work, I can now recognize the triggers and the fears. We need to be honest with ourselves. Instead of pointing the finger at other people, we must examine ourselves. What fears drive us? How could they potentially ruin an opportunity? What can we do to proactively combat those fears? Remember, work is required. Fears aren't going to just fade away because there is a second chance. Deep-rooted fears will only heal as we do the hard work.

If you watched season one of *Last Chance U*, more than likely you immediately fell in love with Ronald Ollie. This guy is one of the most lovable individuals I have ever had the privilege of knowing. Ollie was raised in Shubuta, Mississippi. According to *City-Data .com*, 416 people live in this rural town. In 2017, the median income was $25,617. Ollie's story is one that will rip your heart right out of your chest. When he was a young child, only five years old, his father shot his mother and then killed himself. All of a sudden, in a trailer park in the middle of nowhere, this little boy was an orphan. He was raised by other family members and hadn't really seen enough hope in his life to have a dream. Then he received a football scholarship and had an opportunity to go to college, something he had probably never thought possible. The drive from Shubuta to Scooba was only an hour and nine minutes. He would play football at EMCC for two years, while attending classes. On the first day of class his sophomore year, I sent him to the bookstore to buy his books, and he returned to my office with headphones. I wanted to grab his hand and the headphones and march him right back to the bookstore. But instead, something inside me told me to just embrace the headphones. We had a moment where I tried them on and nodded my head to the rap music blaring in my ear. (Don't worry, he eventually got his books, too.) Ollie wanted to play football at Auburn. That became his dream. As his sophomore year was winding down and his scholarship offers started rolling in, Auburn wasn't one of them. His first offer came from Southeast Missouri State University (SEMO for short). SEMO is located in Cape Girardeau, Missouri, a five-and-a-half-hour drive—or a quick flight. The coaches wanted Ollie to take an official visit to campus. He would have to fly.

Since the day I had met Ronald Ollie, I knew how valuable it would be for him to receive another scholarship when his days at EMCC were done. Community college is only two years. A student takes his or her core required classes to graduate with an associate degree. I knew Ollie needed to buy himself two additional years of having a roof over his head, a bed, regular meals, and support to build his dream. He needed that time as much as he needed the education and the football. He may not have seen that deep into the offer, but I did. It was life or death, success or failure for him.

He received the offer from SEMO, but this was not the end of the story. Not long after, I was checking Twitter before bed when I saw Ollie had tweeted the recruiting coach, "Thanks, but no thanks." I almost fell out of my bed!

The next day, I called him into my office, thinking to myself *Had he lost his mind?* "Here is an opportunity for you to have a place to live for two more years and you are tweeting no thank you?!" I said. Now I felt close to losing *my* mind. "Ollie, what is this about?" I continued. "Why would you turn this offer down when it's the only one you have?"

As the conversation continued, he finally revealed the real reason he had declined the offer: "Ms. Wagner, I don't want to fly. I am afraid to fly."

His fear was holding him back. After we talked it through, he agreed to face his fear and make the trip. "But, Ms. Wagner," he said, "if something happens to me, it's going to be your fault."

"That's okay, Ollie," I replied, "because nothing is going to happen to you."

"You're right. Because I have my headphones."

Fear and Pride: Twin Dream Derailers

Fear is real. But the story we make up about the worst

With Ronald Ollie on his Senior Day at Nicholls State University.

possible outcome may not be. Sometimes we can easily identify the feeling as fear and sometimes it dresses up in another costume to trick us into externally placing the blame on something or someone else. Facing it takes honesty and bravery but also maximizes our opportunities. So grab your headphones, pencils, and your guts and go for it.

Maybe fear isn't the main issue. Maybe it's pride. Like Ollie, maybe we desperately wanted to play at Auburn but our ability is more on the level of SEMO. When you have worked your whole life to perfect a talent, or taken a leap on a big dream, it is a tough pill to swallow when we aren't quite the big deal we thought we were. As an academic counselor, I wanted to be realistic about a student's abilities without killing the dream. I often found myself conflicted over how honest I needed to be. Once I had a track-and-field student-athlete who wanted to be a doctor. He was suffering his way through the pre-med curriculum and it was miserable for everyone involved. We had called him in several times to talk to him about his classes, his grades, and his chosen major. He wasn't budging. He wanted to be a doctor, but he could not pass general biology. Nothing anybody said seemed to be sinking in. Then I watched another counselor use an interesting method to give the student a dose of reality.

We called him in and lay two transcripts on the desk in front of him. The names of the students on each transcript had been cut off. We told him that, hypothetically, his father was in the hospital and needed emergency surgery. His dad had asked that he choose the surgeon. There were two choices. The only information we had on each candidate was their college transcript. He could take a few minutes to look over each transcript and then we needed his decision. It didn't take him long. He grabbed the "A" student's transcript and said, "This one for sure! The other person couldn't even pass general biology. He ain't operating on my dad!"

Perfectly executed and well played! "That is *your* transcript! We're going to need you to pick a new major."

Human beings can be very stubborn. We get so stuck on our own grand ideas that we don't even realize we are digging our own hole with an unrealistic dream. Of course, there are times when we toss in the towel way too early. But there are also times where we hang on way too long. Having a clear view of ourselves and our desired path forward leads to empowerment.

Success comes when we are realistic with ourselves about our abilities, talents, and capacity. My former student wanted to be a doctor. While his dream was not that far-fetched, he wasn't being realistic about his ability to grasp it. Changing his major didn't mean he was dumb. He needed to do it because the entire situation—from the adjustment to college life far away from home to the demands of being a track athlete in a top program to taking on challenging pre-med classes—wasn't working. The circumstances were squashing the opportunity. He needed a reality check.

Then again, many great accomplishments weren't realistic until someone accomplished them. Why can't that someone be you? Many things that are reality today once seemed impossible. In the horse-and-buggy days of the 1800s, cars didn't seem realistic. A metal machine moving seventy miles per hour with a push of a pedal? Crazy! Until it was done. Even in my lifetime, reality has changed as people innovate and create. When I was in college, it was not realistic—or even possible—to do online research on a computer. I had to walk to the campus library, search through the card catalog, find the books, read them, and photocopy pages to get my hands on the information I needed. The Internet was not reality—until someone made it so! Be honest with yourself and then—with a positive realism that's not afraid to dream big—adjust and achieve. Reality is not reality until you create it!

Sharpen Up!

Get out a pen and paper and answer this question: *What do I want?* For example, "I want to be in a stable relationship," "I want to get promoted at work," "I want to get my art in a gallery," etc. Be specific about the opportunity you're looking for and why you want it.

Focus on the opportunity. Find subtle ways to prepare yourself for what you want. Our thoughts control our actions and attitudes. If we believe our dreams can happen, we are more likely to have the tenacity to knock on doors and continue forward instead of quitting. Visualize your opportunity, talk about it as if it is going to happen (or already has), and then do things to keep moving toward the goal. Keep your heart and eyes open, and show up so you can recognize potential opportunities when they appear. For example, go on a date, exceed expectations in your workplace, or call art galleries to inquire on their policies for displaying artwork.

Feel what you feel and move on. Accept and feel all emotions—positive or negative—but give yourself a timeline. When time is up, move on and evaluate the opportunity from a logical standpoint, doing your best to take the emotion out of it. Write down your analysis of the opportunity and fact-check yourself to see if your observations are based on emotion or truth. You may also want to make an old-fashioned pros and cons list.

Create an Opportunity Chart. Across the top of the page (using what follows as an example), list your five non-negotiables. In the left-hand column, list potential opportunities. Place a check mark in the columns where desires align. Notice which opportunity receives the most check marks. The key is to be brutally honest with yourself and stay focused on what you want. Below is a recruiting chart that you can use as a sample for how to make an Opportunity Chart.

RECRUITING CHART SAMPLE

	Immediate Playing Time	Close to Home	TV Exposure	Coaching Philosophy	Academics
Ohio State University			✔		
University of Kentucky	✔	✔	✔	✔	✔
Auburn University		✔	✔		✔
University of Southern California	✔			✔	
Penn State University	✔				✔

Analyzing Your Opportunities

If you rank the schools based on the number of check marks to indicate "yes," Kentucky is the clear winner with all five needs met.

Auburn follows with three, USC and Penn State tie with two, and Ohio State falls last with only one nonnegotiable met. This will be enough for some of you. *Kentucky it is!* If there is still uncertainty, eliminate the lowest-ranking opportunities. In this example, I would eliminate the bottom three since they are each only meeting two needs or fewer. Then start over and redo the chart with the opportunities you have remaining. Since you now have fewer choices, you are forced to look at the top two schools for every category. This will help you make a more confident decision.

Narrowing Down Your Non-negotiables

You may also rank the five non-negotiables in order of importance. Are there one or two that are really more important than the others? For example, you may care more about immediate playing time than living close to home. If what you really want more than anything is immediate contribution to a team, you may be able to sacrifice the desire of being near home to embrace immediate contribution.

Believe in yourself and take the leap!

CHAPTER 5
We All Make Mistakes

"Be brave enough to claim it and humble
enough to learn from it!"

—UNKNOWN

W hen I first met Dakota Allen, he impressed me with his firm handshake and self-assurance as he looked me in the eye. He projected confidence without being cocky, showing that he knew his value and self-worth. He was also respectful and humble. I didn't know why he'd been knocked down to junior college from a Division I school. I had a rule—*never google a player*. I learned this the hard way. I looked up a player once, and after I learned what he'd done to land himself at EMCC, I couldn't get it out of my head, which made me less effective at helping him. I had no idea why Dakota Allen stood in front of me that day. He certainly looked the part of a Power Five football player and acted the part of an upstanding young man. Yet no Division I player I knew came to Scooba by choice, so I knew there had to be a reason.

One look at Dakota's transcripts from Texas Tech confirmed my suspicions. He was a straight-A student. I mean, *complete* As in engineering, one of the most difficult majors known to man. He even passed *calculus* with an A! It wasn't until his last semester of enrollment at Texas Tech that I saw a significant shift—from straight As to Ds and Fs overnight. That was my clue. I knew something happened either right before or during that semester to send him into a tailspin. Straight-A students don't start flunking out without some major life change or shake-up. I was eventually tipped off by one of the producers of *Last Chance U*. It was only then that I saw Dakota's mug shot, the look on his face so different from the warm, personable, hardworking guy I knew. The young man in that picture looked so defeated, so sad, so devalued.

Early on in the semester, Dakota told me his story, in his own words, before I read it on the Internet. I don't remember exactly what he said, but he didn't sugarcoat it. He told me how he and some of his Texas Tech teammates burglarized a house. They broke in and stole TVs and a gun safe. He said the safe was so heavy, he and the other two players involved in the incident struggled to get it out of the house. I remember thinking to myself, *Well, why didn't you just give up and leave it?* They wanted the guns inside badly enough to invest all their strength and mental energy to take them. It wasn't until one of his teammates tried to resell one of the guns that law enforcement eventually connected the dots.

Dakota certainly wasn't proud of his mistakes, but he owned them. So many athletes I worked with previously never really owned their mistakes. There was always an excuse or a justification—someone else to blame. Dakota didn't see it that way. He owned every piece of what he did. He even admitted that as he was robbing the house, he knew he shouldn't be doing it. While I could tell he was grateful for this second chance, I could also tell he absolutely couldn't believe this was where his life had taken him.

Dakota wanted redemption. He wanted a shot to play Division I football again, but, in that moment, I don't think he believed he deserved it. Not because he wasn't good enough athletically, but because he believed his misstep justified losing out on a second chance. He'd had his shot and was convinced that no one would ever trust him with another one again. He let his bad decision control his mood and his outlook on life. I wanted to help him see that he could work past that. I looked him in the eye one day and said, "Dakota, you are better than your worst mistake. Don't let it define or control you." I'm not sure he truly believed me in that moment, but he nodded his head like maybe he would one day.

Over the next year he slowly began to believe that he *was* better than his mistake. Dakota quickly became a leader at EMCC. He wasn't like a lot of the other guys; he had a maturity about him that others didn't have. He wasn't just a leader on the field but off the field as well. He tutored some of his teammates in math—a subject that came easily to him. Literature wasn't his favorite class, but he showed up for reading sessions with his other teammates and encouraged them to listen and think more deeply about the text. He was a favorite among the faculty—and, quite frankly, myself. After righting his ship, Dakota was allowed to return to Texas Tech University for his last two years of college. He became a team captain his senior year, graduated early, and began work toward his master's degree. When he received an invite to the NFL Scouting Combine, the weeklong showcase where teams evaluate college football players, there was talk about his character. In an interview written by Aaron Wilson and published on April 21, 2019, in the *Houston Chronicle*, Dakota discussed his past and his approach to the Combine with candor:

> I'm just straight up with them. [. . .] I tell them exactly what I did. I own it 100 percent, and I also tell them what I've learned from it. I tell them I grew as a person. I learned a lot about the people around me. I hope that they'll give me an opportunity, because I won't let them down. I've learned a lot through that situation. Most importantly, I learned how to handle adversity.

In the end, Dakota got his redemption and was selected in the seventh round of the 2019 NFL draft by the Los Angeles Rams. After a very successful preseason with the Rams, he was signed as a roster player for his rookie season with the Oakland Raiders and is now with the Jacksonville Jaguars.

With Dakota before his last college football game at Texas Tech University.

You Are Better Than Your Worst Mistake

There are thousands of stories just like Dakota's. We all make mistakes every day, from little tiny ones to great big ones we think we can never recover from. But mistakes are inevitable! And while we tend to excuse the smaller-scale missteps that happen on a daily basis, we often beat ourselves up for the ones that change the trajectory of our lives even if they don't make headlines. I'll say it again for the people in the back: Mistakes are *inevitable*, but we can learn to have compassion for ourselves no matter the size or magnitude of our slipups.

We have previously established that I love pencils—in fact, my brand depends upon them! Why do I love them more than any other writing utensil, you ask? Because they have erasers. I think the mere fact that the eraser exists proves that mistakes are *supposed* to happen. When writing with a pencil, we give ourselves the opportunity to catch our mistakes as we move along. We don't fixate on the mishaps; we simply erase and replace. We don't count the eraser particles or keep a chart to track our mess ups. We just blow it off and move on. As with our writing, so it is in life. When we make a mistake, we can acknowledge it with an "Oops!" correct it, and move on.

We must own our mistakes, yet many of us only make a half-hearted attempt at this. We acknowledge the error while using the conjunction that completely wipes away the acknowledgment—"BUT." Someone once told me that when you use "but" in a sentence, you're devaluing what you stated before the "but." For example: I like you a lot, but I don't think it will work out. The real message: I *don't* like you; I am just trying to be nice and not hurt your feelings. We will halfway admit that we were wrong, but we tend to let ourselves off the hook by ultimately blaming something or somebody else. To completely own the mistake means we just own it. There is a period at the end of the apology instead of a comma.

When we follow up an "acknowledgment" with an excuse or blame someone else, we aren't totally owning our mess up. Social researcher and author Brené Brown studied blame and came to the conclusion that we point the finger at others for our own mishaps in order to release pain and discomfort. It is easier to pour our energy into assigning fault than to be accountable to ourselves. Brown states in her book, *Daring Greatly*, "Blame is simply the discharge of pain and discomfort. We blame when we're uncomfortable and experience pain—when we're vulnerable, angry, hurt, in shame, grieving. There's nothing productive about blame, and it often involves shaming someone or just being mean."

What good does placing blame do us? I'll answer, speaking from my own experience—nothing! Telling someone off makes us feel good in the short term but that's where it ends. A much better solution is to simply sit for a few minutes and process the news before responding. Ask yourself the following questions:

- What did I contribute to this situation?

- What about this situation has nothing to do with me?

- Is there a solution here?

- What boundaries can I put in place to prevent this from happening again?

Oftentimes, we make the very best decision we can make in that moment. Sometimes, raging is absolutely my best reaction. Hear me out—it is not *the* best response, but it is *my* best reaction in that moment given the situation or circumstance. Instead of beating ourselves up, we can acknowledge that, given the situation, we did the best we could. We might have hurt someone else in the process and that needs acknowledgment, but inside the exact moment we probably aren't capable of recognizing the hurt we caused nor are we capable of addressing it genuinely. This comes later, after the raw emotion leaves, when we have space to reevaluate our actions. Rather that day, we gave all we had to give. It doesn't excuse the mistake, but it does allow us to have compassion for ourselves.

Here is a very transparent example of this: I was married to a man I adored and had a beautiful, perfect, six-month-old baby. Life was grand (or so I thought)! I'd let my guard down with my husband and become vulnerable. I wasn't a jealous person; I didn't question him—he had complete freedom because I "knew" beyond a shadow of a doubt that he loved me and would never jeopardize our relationship. For four years, the thought of him cheating on me literally never crossed my mind.

Then in 2008, after our daughter was born, it all came crashing down. I remember being suspicious of some strange activity on his cell phone. Yet as soon as the accusation entered my mind, I turned it around on myself, beating myself up over my "crazy" thinking. Gradually, those suspicions grew as his activities became more obvious. I would ask him about it, and he came up with the *worst* excuses. The repeated "unknown caller" in the middle of the night was a "telemarketer." He arrived at home two hours later than normal because of traffic. (On a deserted highway. In rural Mississippi.) But the cycle remained the same. I believed him, quickly dismissed my worries, and moved on. Then one day I logged into our AT&T account and looked at the itemized list of text messages and phone calls he was making. My heart sank. I *knew*. The proof was there in black and white. I called the number anyway, and my heartache was confirmed. I heard her voice and quickly hung up, dropping to my knees in utter disbelief.

He was *cheating* on me. How could this happen? How did I *let* this happen? I was *devastated*. Was my marriage over? I didn't want my marriage to be over. I picked up the phone and called my best friend, Tiffany. She could hardly make out what I was saying through my screaming and uncontrollable sobbing. She lived in another state, but she was so worried about me being alone that she considered driving to me right then and there. I wouldn't allow it—she was a lawyer with a high-stress job and a family of her own. "Then get it together," she said. She was right. I had to make a plan. I couldn't just sit around and cry for weeks. I had to gather evidence and confront him. I think I have blocked out that actual encounter with my ex-husband—it's too painful, I suppose. But I do remember his complete denial, despite the mounds of evidence I had to the contrary. He admitted to talking to his former girlfriend too frequently. He admitted to connecting emotionally but denied any physical involvement or actual affair. I knew better.

From that moment on, I went into mama bear mode in a futile effort to protect my family. I got angry at him, got angry at her, went to counseling, quit counseling, uprooted my family, compromised my morals, tried to ignore reality, woke up, got a plan, and then I left him. I made 999 mistakes during those three years, but looking back, I was doing the very best I could in that moment.

The very act of placing blame is what led to my desperation. I wanted to prove it was his fault or her fault—that *I* was blameless. I wanted to keep score. I wanted to punish him. These are, of course, very normal reactions for a spouse going through this type of trauma. However, if I'd had the ability to process what was happening without needing to place blame or punish, maybe I could have led our family in a different direction. I'll never know for sure, but it's safe to say I lost myself for a while. Only after we attended counseling together did I realize that our marriage was truly over. Our priorities were simply not aligned. My top priority was my daughter, followed closely by my husband and the rest of my family. His top priority was himself. After I had grasped at every straw possible, I faced reality, took control of the situation, and called an attorney to discuss filing for divorce. By taking back control, I was able to learn from my own mistakes and move forward to face the reality that my "family" was going to look differently than I'd envisioned.

While my ex-husband ultimately made the big mistake that ended our marriage, I also had to own my contribution to the situation and acknowledge that my behavior spiraled out of control. It took me a while to get there, but eventually I could recognize and verbalize that we both held responsibility for our marriage ending. And while I owned my part, I developed compassion for myself and even for my ex-husband, recognizing that we *both* did the best we could, given our individual struggles.

Don't Be Sorry, Be Good

In high school, I was a member of my high school's award-winning show choir, Attaché. (Think: a much cooler version of *Glee*.) This wasn't your average show choir. This was *the* winningest show choir in the country—National Champions, baby! We were phenomenal! This pride of Mississippi produced many notable individuals, including NSYNC member Lance Bass, Broadway performer Heath Calvert, country music star Shelly Fairchild, and drummer Keith Carlock. And me, of course. We practiced relentlessly with a level of discipline and zeal that was quite frankly ridiculous for teenagers to exhibit.

The talent within this group was amazing. To be in the back row was an accomplishment in itself, but a spot in the front row meant you had *really* made it. I would have dreams about performing in the front row (or nightmares, really). I wanted to be in the front row *so* badly. All forty of the singer/dancers would be onstage waiting for the choreographer to call their name during our blocking practice. On one particular day, we had gone through three of the four rows, and my name still hadn't been called. Could *I* be in the front row? Was I really good enough to be front and center? Then our director called my name: Brittany Wagner. YES! Front row! I had done it.

As we started to run through the first number, I unexpectedly froze. Mental block. I lost it—all of it. I forgot the dance moves, the blocking, and the notes. The piano stopped. All the instruments stopped. And our director, Mr. Fehr, jumped from the pit below to the stage with a single leap. He came straight for me, got in my face, and yelled, "What are you doing?!"

"I don't know. I'm sorry," I said, my face turning bright red.

"Don't be sorry, be good!" he said back to me—calmly but firmly —looking me dead in the eye.

Those words motivated me; they allowed me to own my power. I felt a fire in my soul. Yes, sir, I *will* be good. And from that moment on, I was. I made plenty more mistakes. I fell onstage, sang the wrong

Performing with my award-winning high school show choir, Attaché.

Reminiscing with Mr. David Fehr, third from right.

words, threw up the wrong jazz hand at the wrong time, but I never cowered in response to a mistake again. I owned my mistake, kept smiling, and kept going. When we value ourselves and have confidence in our abilities and who we are, we don't sit in our mistakes very long. Self-worth allows us to pull ourselves up by our bootstraps, check ourselves, let go of our mistakes, and move on.

The ability to own the mistake and respond appropriately, coupled with the self-worth to stand back up and "be good," breaks the cycle of repeating the same mistake over and over again. Have you heard the saying, "God throws a pebble, then a stone, and then a brick"?

If we don't learn from the mistake the first time around, the pebble becomes a stone, and so on. Eventually, mistakes repeated have the ability to damage us and others in ways that can take longer to repair. The moral of the story? We can't really accept our mistake if we repeat the same patterns of behavior over and over. Being truly sorry means breaking the cycle of behavior and aiming to do better in the future.

Here is the cold, hard truth. The mistakes you make and the consequences you suffer will not go away until the lesson is learned. What step are you on? The pebble, the stone, or the brick? How many more times will you allow yourself to be pummeled by the same exact circumstance? The consequences will only get bigger, the hole will only get deeper, and the effect will only become more detrimental. We have the ability to take a different course of action and walk on a different path by learning from our mistakes.

I believe taking action helps us to start taking steps on our new path. Here are several helpful activities that have worked for me in letting go of past mistakes and regaining confidence as I embarked on a new path. Remember, we cannot let go of something that we refuse to take ownership of! Own the mistake, understand the situation you were in when you made it, and then begin the process of forgiving yourself and others involved. When you are ready, try some of the following exercises.

Light the Fire

1. Write your mistake on a sheet of paper.

2. Go to a safe, non-flammable area where you are permitted to burn with a matchbook or lighter.

3. Hold the "mistake" with both hands and be silent. Breathe

very intently and slowly, in and out. Take a few minutes to think about yourself and this time in your life.

4. Then, light the corner of the sheet of paper on fire with the match or lighter. Hold it as long as you can safely while it burns.

5. When you have to release it, say out loud, "I give myself permission to let go of _____ " or "I am forgiven and moving on." Verbalize your letting go.

This can take any form you want; these are just suggestions. The point is to release it. Allow yourself to feel the emotions of letting it go. Once all you have left are ashes, celebrate this new beginning. I have done this with the ending of relationships, situations where I messed up, and entire time periods in my life when I just wasn't being my best self.

Put a Pencil to It

I love to journal. When we write down our feelings, we allow ourselves to get honest about our mistakes, pain, struggles, and shame. Allow yourself to free write about your mistake for at least five minutes with no agenda. This is not going to be published writing, so don't get preoccupied with writing "well." The point is simply to release the emotions and get them out of you.

Make Amends

Sometimes, we may have harmed someone else with our mistake. If so, it may be best to make amends and write the other person a letter, too. It is up to you whether you actually mail it or not, but the therapy will come in writing it. I can't tell you the number of times

I have written letters that were never mailed. I also have realized my own wrongs in reading these letters when I was better able to process the entire story.

Step Nine of the Alcoholics Anonymous program is all about making amends. Page eighty-three of *The Twelve Steps and Twelve Traditions* states, "The readiness to take the full consequences of our past acts, and to take responsibility for the well-being of others at the same time, is the very spirit of Step Nine."

AA breaks down amends into three categories:

Direct Amends: Taking personal responsibility for your actions and confronting the person you would like to reconcile with.

Indirect Amends: Finding ways to repair damage that cannot be reversed or undone, by doing things like volunteering and helping others.

Living Amends: When you show others as well as yourself that you have made a genuine lifestyle change and discarded previous destructive behaviors and patterns. In doing so, you are making a commitment to yourself and those you have hurt to live a better life from this point on.

Making direct amends is a good first step to owning a mistake and apologizing. And although *we* may be ready to make amends, we have to consider that the other person may not be ready to receive them. This is why I suggest making direct amends in a letter rather than in person or over the phone. Allow the other person the space needed to process and respond. Good old-fashioned snail mail allows that space.

When taking this amends-making process a step further into living amends, we realize that our actions have to match our words. When our words and actions don't match, manipulation is taking place. In an active relationship, be prepared to back up your words with actions. If you're making direct amends, state the intended actions in your apology. Apologize in detail for what you did, explain why or how that action came about, and then very specifically state how you are going to correct that behavior.

When we make a mistake (big or small), we can learn from it to then create a better future. That is the purpose of mishaps, of mistakes—to help us grow. We will manifest the same things in our lives until we learn from them. We will continue to attract the same energy we put out into the world until we change our modus operandi. We will make the same decisions over and over until we learn how to make new ones. If we never learn that the stove is hot and make the decision not to touch it, we will keep repeating that behavior over and over until it burns our hand off. Don't beat yourself up over your mistakes—recognize them, acknowledge them, and learn from them. We become better because of our mistakes and do better in the future because we *know* better.

Mistakes are tricky, but learning the lessons life throws at us is key to making the most of a second chance. I think at some point we are given the wisdom and the willpower to heal ourselves. Maybe the consequences of the repeated mistake become too detrimental. Maybe we just become wiser. But when we are ready, it will click, and we will have developed the character traits needed to make the most of our next chance. We will look at what we have done and commit to never doing it again. That doesn't remove the temptation or remove all the obstacles. Life doesn't suddenly become sunshine and rainbows once we make our decision to change, but something happens inside ourselves when we are truly ready to learn from our mistakes and move forward. And once we've made this change, we can be certain that we will be ready for our second chance opportunity, however and whenever it comes.

Sharpen Up!

Get a plan. What do you need to do in order to move on from this mistake? Be specific. Write it all down and then go back and list the items from those that are easiest to tackle to those hardest to accomplish. Give yourself a timeline and start. Cross the items off as you complete them and celebrate your achievements.

Acknowledge the situation you were in when you made the decision leading to the mishap. What are you going to do to prevent yourself from being in that situation again or responding the same way when you are in it? And who can offer you tough love, accountability, and support in those moments?

How you respond after the mistake occurs matters most. Make amends where necessary, identify the lesson you needed to learn, and commit to making a lifestyle change.

CHAPTER 6
Somebody Likin' Ya

"Life's a game, all you have to do
is know how to play it."

—UNKNOWN

"Do you have a pencil?" may be the one-liner everyone associates with me and my time on *Last Chance U*, but I may have actually imparted the greatest wisdom of my career when I screamed, "Half the battle is just somebody likin' ya!" to a group of football players. It happened during our first academic meeting of the year in season two of the show. I did not prepare the line ahead of time; it just came to me in that moment.

My next words followed quickly: "It's easy to flunk an asshole!"

Remember that jerk in high school or college who would walk into class late every day, take his seat in the back of the room, and sleep, clown around, or complain his way through the entire hour? Maybe he wore a hat low to cover his disengaged eyes or played on his phone.

If he did participate, he was annoying, sarcastic, or acted like he had better things to do. He may have been a nice guy otherwise, but in the classroom setting, no one liked him—especially not the teacher.

I've worked with a number of such students during my career, and they are somehow always baffled at the end of the semester when their grade is below what they think they deserve. That's where the phrase, "It's easy to flunk an asshole," comes into play. Teachers are human beings, too. When calculating final grades, staring at a border-line situation between a C or a D grade, teachers become even more human. Suddenly their brain is filled with images of this dude in the back row, giving little to no effort. Without any positive relational equity, it's awfully easy for the instructor to submit the *D*. In contrast, I've witnessed numerous exceptions made for students who are struggling but putting forth effort. In the game of life, people like nice people. And because we are all human beings, sometimes nice people get breaks that the assholes of the world don't get. It's that simple—just be a nice person.

Some people don't realize they have tendencies that make them unlikeable. They aren't trying to be jerks; they just don't have enough awareness about their behavior to know that they're coming across that way. Sitting in the back row scrolling through Instagram while a professor is delivering a lecture is disrespectful and does not help your cause come grading time.

I've worked with athletes who genuinely were not jerks, but they didn't see the value in winning over their teachers. In fact, they had no idea how to even accomplish that. I made it my mission to teach them. My step-by-step lesson went something like this:

Step one: Go to class. Show up every day, on time.

Step two: Be prepared. Show up with needed materials.

Step three: Make eye contact with the teacher and nod your head three times while he or she is talking.

"What do I nod my head at?" students would ask.

"I don't care. Just nod your head three times during the class period as if you do care," I said.

Step four: Hold your pencil in your hand and write something on the paper.

"What am I writing?"

"Again, I don't care," I said. "Doodle your name; write me a sweet note. It doesn't matter."

After a student had practiced this method for a couple of weeks, two things happened. I would enter the teacher's lounge and hear instructors having positive conversations about these athletes. "He's coming to class and listening. He is even taking notes! I just love that he is trying so hard."

I would smile to myself. It was working. When it comes to relational equity, perception is reality. By playing along with what a student is "supposed to do," the athlete was impressing his teacher and winning the likeability game. The instructors appreciated the behavior and began to root for the athlete.

Ironically, the second thing that happened was the athlete began forming good classroom habits. It may have started out as fake, but, in time, as the athlete pretended to listen, he would find himself *actually* listening. These athletes became interested in what they were learning and began to genuinely participate in class. Over time the athlete was no longer exhibiting likeable classroom behaviors, he was actually engaging in them!

See Yourself as Others See You

Hear this: I'm not suggesting selling out who you are to embrace behaviors deemed acceptable by society. But I am suggesting you have awareness of yourself, those around you, and how your behavior can help or hurt you in various situations. There are behaviors deemed acceptable in classrooms, in boardrooms, and in living rooms. Adapting to display those behaviors—and be a likeable person—is not being fake. It's being smart. I am not the first person to see a powerful connection between being likeable and being successful, both personally and professionally. There's a reason Dale Carnegie's book *How to Win Friends & Influence People,* first published in 1936, has sold more than 15 million copies and become a timeless bestseller. Choosing to present yourself in a positive way is a way of advocating for yourself and can open up greater opportunities. Let's dive into some of the marks of a likeable person.

Someone recently asked me what quality I deemed the most important for a person to possess. I gave a cookie cutter answer, something like "honesty," because I wasn't sure of my real answer. I had never considered it before. As I ruminated on it later and kept a mental tally of qualities and how different ones affected me and others, I came to this answer. The quality I think is most valuable for a person to possess is *awareness*. There is a respect for oneself and others that comes along with awareness that is highly likeable.

This quality allows us to more effectively prepare for and adjust to new environments. How can we remain gracious in challenging daily situations? Here are a few characteristics of likeable people:

Likeable people stay in their own lanes. Raise your hand if you grew up in a small town. If you didn't, let me paint the picture for you. In a small town (especially a Southern one) everybody's business is, well…everybody's business. Drama abounds because everyone has her hand in the pot—and everyone's stirring it. That can be one downfall of a small town. No one stays in their lane.

Whether we call them "busybodies," "nosy Nellies," or "drama queens," those who meddle in the business of others lack likeability. Others aren't drawn to them—except for maybe a juicy morsel of gossip. Social media has given this type of person an even larger arena in which to play. Social media shaming is a real thing as people hide behind their keyboards and type whatever spills into their heads.

Having a Facebook account does not qualify a person as an expert in how others should parent their children, navigate relationships, vote in an election, or take care of their personal appearance. People in my neighborhood have even taken to Facebook to complain about one another's lawn-care maintenance. This is social media shaming. And it is not okay. Likeable people stay in their own lane. The stress of constant drama can be debilitating. We create drama when we swerve into the next lane without an invitation to do so. And let's face it—when we are focused on someone else's life, we are getting sidetracked from our own.

I recently viewed a cute video on TikTok with a toddler telling his mother to "worry 'bout yourself." The video went viral because of the voice of the toddler looking at his mother and responding with such a grown-up comment. However, maybe it *really* went viral because we needed to hear it. Stay in your own lane and…worry 'bout yourself.

Likeable people create a safe environment. I recently heard the first feeling we attach to as a small child is safety—or the feeling of being safe. From our earliest days as an infant, one of the ways we are made to feel safe is by the tone in a person's voice. Babies recognize a soothing tone and associate it with a feeling of safety. The same is true for adults. We want to feel secure in our environments and relationships. And just like babies, the tone in which we are spoken to most of the time has more value than the actual words.

A harsh tone can immediately trigger warning signals in our brains and bodies. Flashing red lights that scream, *This person is not safe! Abort! Abort!* The feeling of not being safe may cause a fight, flight, or freeze reaction. If we want to be likeable, we must be aware of our tone and adjust it to be one of safety. Think about some of the greatest voices of our time: Morgan Freeman, James Earl Jones, Mr. Rogers, and Oprah. Each of these voices is inviting and comforting. Likeable people speak in a likeable tone. We are more able to hear and process the words being said when the speaker delivers those words in a non-threatening way.

Matching energy levels is another way to create safety in your communication and build trust. I have a friend who is super high energy. Her energy is genuine, but she can blow people away with her overzealous happiness and loud, shrill voice. That energy level can be intimidating and even abrasive to a person who can't match it. And unfortunately, someone who has the potential to be truly likeable has become the opposite due to her inability to gauge the energy of those to whom she is speaking.

When you're likeable, there are fewer negative preconceived notions. In Chapter 5, I mentioned one of my "Advising 101" rules: Never google a player. While this rule saved the day when it came to my relationship-building efforts with Dakota Allen, I had to learn it the hard way. I made this rule for myself following a huge mistake. I found out that a "Five-Star" Division I player was getting the boot from a university in my home state. The coaches at my institution were doing their best to swoop him up and bring him to the "Books-and-Ball Rehab Center" down the road. (We called it that because there was nothing else to do but study and play football in that tiny town.) I googled him and called the counselor at the school that had kicked him out. I wanted to know everything I could about this young man I was going to be working with.

As you might expect, his previous school had nothing positive to say. He was aggressive. He hated women. He was unstable. He didn't respect authority. I was afraid of the guy before he ever got to campus. I had already made up my mind about the horrible person he was, and I treated him in line with that. I lost my ability to help him because I couldn't un-hear and un-read the information I *thought* I needed to know.

When we have preconceived notions and judgments about a person, we don't allow that individual to tell his or her own narrative. In fact, that information fundamentally changes our attitude toward the person, who may need our help. We limit our ability to meet someone where they are, build rapport, and grow them from exactly where they are.

We all pass judgment at times, both knowingly and unknowingly. We see that person in the grocery store and turn down another aisle. We see that person pop up on our screen and send the call to voicemail. And because we have already formed a negative opinion, we close ourselves off from any positive interactions with them. Those who are

liked by others keep an open mind, accept people, and allow them
to tell their own narrative. When we dismiss someone based on our
preconceived notions, what we are actually doing is admitting that we
are not capable of handling her story. Our own insecurities prevent us
from meeting another person where she is. We don't trust ourselves
enough to hear the truth in real time and respond with grace and love,
so we make it up so we don't have to deal with it at all.

**Likeable people avoid the triggers of difficult
people.** Working with college coaches is no piece of cake. Most head
coaches have ego-driven personalities. Some, I would argue, have multiple traits of narcissistic personality disorder. This control-hungry,
demanding way of life is what makes them winners in the game of
sport. The head coach at East Mississippi was a winner on the field.
He could also tear down a room in one second and walk away smiling.

After working with him for several years, I started showing physical
signs of anxiety and stress that I attribute to how he treated me. My
left eye started twitching uncontrollably whenever I heard his voice or
knew I was going to have to interact with him. His consistent attitude
and actions toward me over time created stress and anxiety that not
only affected me mentally but physically as well. The student-athletes
with whom I worked were aware of it, which probably strengthened
our relationship even more. Still, this stressful situation was taking
a toll on me. The eye doctor who diagnosed my twitch as a stress-
induced reaction encouraged me to see a therapist. I started therapy
(again) to help me cope with the stress of my job.

Right off the bat, my therapist wanted to work with me on calming
my mindset prior to my interactions with this coach. His first sugges-

tion was to simply change the ringtone on my phone for the coaches who caused me stress. He encouraged me to change my ringtone for these numbers to something soothing, happy, or even funny. "And don't answer on the first ring," he said. "Sit and breathe and listen to the soothing sound before you answer." I was amazed at how this one trick lowered my heartbeat, my voice, and my stress.

Likeable people have empathy. Author Brené Brown says that sympathy and empathy are not the same. Sympathy is feeling sorry for someone—almost as if we are better than them, sitting in a higher spot, looking down, and feeling sorry for their situation. Empathy, on the other hand, is crawling down on the floor with them and doing our best to experience exactly what they are experiencing. Empathy is putting ourselves in someone else's shoes. As I mentioned in an earlier chapter, behavior is never the issue; it's the symptom.

Whenever I encounter someone exhibiting cruel or unhealthy behavior, I repeat this phrase to myself: *I am sorry for whatever has happened to you for you to be this angry.* (Substitute "angry" with hateful, dishonest, mean-spirited, passive, rude—there are many cruel and unhealthy behaviors that arise from deep-seated anger.) Sometimes I whisper the phrase to myself. Other times I have said it out loud directly to the offending person. I feel it is important to acknowledge to the individual that this behavior is not who he or she is; it is a symptom of deeper issues.

The truth is, most people's spirits have been broken. Everywhere we go, people are showing up with years of trauma, pain, sadness, and stress—or even one really bad day. And while it doesn't excuse their bad behavior, acknowledging their pain can help us show empathy and kindness.

Repeated acts of empathy, kindness, and understanding change people. Beating someone down and adding more crap to the already very large pile of shit in someone's life won't change anyone. This only amplifies the negative stories they're telling themselves. But to flip the script and show someone compassion in a moment when they might not even deserve it—that can change people. Empathy changes people. I previously mentioned the stress the head coach caused in my life when I worked with him. He also had moments of remarkable compassion. I had to work late a lot; college athletics is not a nine-to-five job. I was selective about what I was willing to work late for, but sometimes doing it was just inevitable.

One evening, the school administration was holding an after-hours meeting to discuss a policy that was negatively affecting students. Our head coach had asked me to prepare a presentation about the effects this policy was having on student-athletes, and present it to the board. I agreed without hesitation. I didn't tell Coach, but this meant I had to hire a babysitter to watch Kennedy while I was working late. I didn't have the extra money to pay the sitter. After the meeting was over, Coach walked over to me and told me I had done a great job and shook my hand. In the handshake was a $100 bill. He looked at me and said, "This is for the babysitter." He didn't just feel sorry for me, he put himself in my shoes. He thought about my situation and what I had to sacrifice to effectively do my job that day. He showed empathy.

Ricky Gervais wrote this quote into his Netflix show, *After Life*: "Happiness is amazing. It is so amazing it doesn't matter if it is yours or not. Good people do things for other people." Happiness is contagious. We can change our own happiness levels by giving to others and witnessing their successes—sharing in a slice of their sunshine.

One of the first schools that hired me for consulting work after *Last Chance U* was a suburban school district outside Detroit, Michigan. I had no idea what to expect. At the time I stepped in, Michigan had done away with zoning. Students no longer attended a school based on attendance boundaries. The idea was to give every student a great education regardless of the neighborhood in which he or she lived. This was a great idea—in theory. However, if a student didn't have involved parents to make the decision and provide transportation to a new school, nothing changed.

Politicians could vote the no-zoning rules in, but without the resources to make it happen, the plan would never work. This particular suburb decided to bus its students in. Students from inner city Detroit rode a bus one hour each way for the chance of a better education and life. Obviously, this wasn't easy. These students made a brave and hard choice to get to this school.

One of these students played football. I watched him eat alone at the cafeteria table day after day and asked a vice principal about his story. I was told he had been nicknamed "Ugly Man." He was basically homeless. He took showers in the locker room after practice, when the coach allowed it. He didn't look like anyone else, smell like anyone else. And he didn't have the educational background anyone else had. He had a name, a real name, but few people knew it. Instead, his peers used that horrible nickname they invented for him; that was the name he heard, and undoubtedly internalized about himself, day after day.

He had two strikes against him for fighting. The school had a "three strikes you're out" policy. When I asked him about his fights and why he would risk such a great opportunity at this new school, he said, "I ride a bus one hour a day one way to get here. I am doing the best I can. I play football in torn-up cleats, I struggle through classes with half the preparation. I am trying. And then, I get made fun of. I have been going to school here for months and no one even knows my name. It's KJ. I take it and I take it and I take it, and then... I hit someone."

Wow! I immediately thought of every kid in America who has a similar story. How and why can we be so cruel to one another? Being likeable means looking around. It means being kind to those who don't look like us, who don't smell like us, who aren't as prepared or knowledgeable as us. Being likeable means eliminating the name-calling, the cheap shots, and, by damn, calling people by their names.

Sharpen Up!

Act like you care. Sometimes you genuinely do care while other times you may be putting on an Oscar-winning performance. Parents know how to play this game. When small children master a skill, even tiny ones, they get extremely excited. Every little accomplishment is a huge deal. The reality is, we as parents don't necessarily share the same level of enthusiasm about all of them. It is not that the accomplishments aren't great—they are. As adults, we have more experience and a larger world-view, so Junior learning to put on his socks isn't something that will make us drop everything for a big celebration. But we act excited anyway. How many of us have featured scribbled art in a prominent spot on our refrigerators or wore a handmade clay necklace with our Sunday best because of our toddler's beaming pride? Even if we don't feel it, we act excited and engaged because we know it is so important to our child. It is the relationship we cherish, not necessarily the art or the skills.

In his book *Caring Enough to Hear and Be Heard,* David W. Augsburger writes: "Being heard is so close to being loved that for the average person, they are almost indistinguishable." In the game of being likeable, acting—in the form of listening and paying attention—is sometimes required. The amazing thing is, in the process of acting, many times we actually start to care. What we think, say, and believe, we become. So what may start out as an acting job might end up as genuine action. Sometimes faking our attitude actually changes our attitude.

Have awareness. Be conscious of yourself and your own needs, wants, and boundaries. You are important and have value. Don't discount your own worth. Take care of you first. But then, be aware of others. They have value, too!

Stay in your lane. In life, there are things we have control over that are ours to handle. And then, there are things we may want to control, we may think we could handle better than someone else—but those things are not ours to handle. Be conscious of what is yours to care for, talk about, and judge. I have heard many times there are three things to think before speaking: Is it true? Is it kind? Is it necessary?

I will add a fourth: Is it any of your business?

Create safety. Feeling safe is a basic human need. How can we create a safe environment for others?

- **Adjust tone and inflection.** You can change the meaning of a sentence simply by changing your inflection or tone of voice. Take, for example, the following statement: "I am not going to buy you a car." Say this sentence out loud several times and put emphasis on different words. The listener can insinuate a different meaning based on the word you emphasize. It is important to be deliberate in the message we want the listener to receive. It might be beneficial to record yourself talking or having a tough conversation and listen back after the emotion has subsided. We tend to hear ourselves more honestly when listening on an external device and outside the difficult situation.

- **Change the pronoun.** The phrases "You need to…," "I need you to…" can feel very demanding and nagging. There is almost no other way to receive them. When talking to college students, I tried to change my pronouns and only use plural pronouns: "we," "us," "our." This seemed to make my words feel less intimidating.

  "We have a quiz in English coming up and we are going to need to set aside some time to study. When can we do that?" By changing a pronoun, and speaking in a calm voice, I decreased students' stress levels and they were more willing to do what I was asking them to do. This is because the student heard: "I am not in this alone. I have help." *She is safe.*

- **Create comfortable spaces.** What does your office or living room look like? Who is it comfortable for? Most of the time, our offices and entertaining areas are comfortable for us but may be uncomfortable for those we invite in. Think about those who come into your space and what puts them at ease. At EMCC, I put intentional effort into making my office colorful and inviting for the athletes. I wanted them to be comfortable in the space and also feel motivated by it. I hung bulletin boards on the walls. I took pictures of athletes at graduation or on game day when they were finally playing for the team they had worked so hard to play for. I would hang these pictures all over the bulletin boards. Current athletes would stand and stare at the accomplishments of those who had stood in the exact same space (literally and figuratively), and persevered. I had countless athletes say to me, "I am gonna be on the bulletin board one day, Ms. Wagner." How can you create a safe space for others to enter into? Other people's safety in your space is important when it comes to connection and relationship-building success!

Keep an open mind and cultivate empathy. Meet people where they are, exactly as they are. Do your best to eliminate preconceived notions due to appearance, manners, communication methods, educational backgrounds, or other factors. Allow people to tell their own stories. When meeting difficult/different people, ask yourself: *What must have happened to them in life for them to be this* _____? Many times, I've found the worse the behavior, the bigger the trauma.

Do your best to not place yourself above them as if you feel sorry for them, but to allow yourself to crawl down in the dungeon with them and stand in their shoes. Perspectives change when we can really see our own selves wrestling through the struggles of others.

Life is about balance. I'm not asking you to sell out who you are in order to be liked. I am also not suggesting you maximize your second chance at the complete cost of those who stand in your way. There is an opportunity for everyone to come out ahead. We can take care of ourselves while also being kind to others. We can think about our needs, while also considering the needs of others. We can like ourselves while also being likeable to others!

CHAPTER 7
Hold On

"Patience is not the ability to wait, but the ability
to keep a good attitude while waiting."
—JOYCE MEYER

He's failed a drug test." The voice on the phone was a coach from a college three hours away and "he" was the quarterback of a Power Five program who had once been one of my student-athletes. But he was more than that. He had also become like a son to me, and he was a human who needed to make good on his life-changing opportunity. So I made time in my schedule and as soon as possible dropped everything, hopped in my car, and made the long drive to the college.

I was fuming the entire drive. How in the world could he do this? He *knows*—every athlete knows—there will be a drug test. Why would you do a drug when you know you're going to have to take a drug test? It's not that complicated.

I picked him up at his apartment and his first words were, "I'm starving. Can we go eat?"

I reluctantly steered the car to a sandwich shop across town. I'd held my tongue, but once he had buckled his seatbelt, I let out my frustration. "How could you be so dumb?" I charged. I launched into the rules of the conference and how he would be kicked off the team and out of school if he failed another one. I reminded him how hard he had worked to get where he was. (I'm sure I also reminded him of how hard *I had worked* to get him there!) My rant must have lasted fifteen minutes, because I was still talking as we pulled into the parking lot of the eatery. I glanced over and his eyes were fixed on the floorboard. He had a blank expression on his face. I asked in a much calmer voice: "Why? Why are you making these decisions?"

"They aren't decisions I'm making," he said. "I am not deciding to ruin my future. I just don't know how *not* to."

"I don't know how to handle the stress and pressure of all of this," he explained. "I don't know what else to do. I don't want to fail another drug test, but I can't function in this stress without the drug. I don't know what else to do to get relief."

His words slapped me across the face. I got it. I felt like an idiot. I was blaming him as if he was doing it on purpose. I knew better. This wasn't a situation of him thinking the rules didn't apply to him or not caring about his future; he had no idea how to *not* do something he had always done. He didn't know how to just sit—and hold on.

My Breakthrough Insight

I have never been an avid reader. I'm not proud of it, but I was the college student who would buy the CliffsNotes version for every book that was "required reading." After graduation, I gradually began to read more. One of the first books I read as an adult that truly impacted me was *A Million Little Pieces* by James Frey.

I love Oprah Winfrey. I don't know her personally, but I still love her. I think I feel a kinship with her because she is from my home state of Mississippi. In my opinion, she is one of the wisest and greatest individuals to have graced this planet. She picked *A Million Little Pieces* as one of her first Oprah Book Club selections. I went out immediately and bought it—because Oprah said to. I sat down to read this memoir, and I sat…and sat…and sat. I could not put it down!

This book moved me like nothing I had ever read. Frey revealed insights into a battle that had touched my life but about which I didn't truly understand—addiction. My grandfather was an alcoholic. I have vivid memories of him getting drunk and watching as my mom had to clean up the mess afterward. I remember the smell of hard liquor and cigarette smoke that permeated his house. But I never comprehended his struggle. I was a little girl. I had no idea all the things he had already been through to take him to the point of numbing out with a bottle of a dark brown liquid. *A Million Little Pieces* gave me insight into a piece of my grandfather's world. At the time I read it, I had no idea I would fall in love with an addict several years later.

A few months after Frey's book came out, a controversy erupted over it. Several publications reported that key parts of the memoir had been greatly exaggerated and even fabricated by Frey. Oprah was mad. She devoted an entire show to an interview with Frey and his publisher. She confronted him, telling him that she felt "duped" and believed he had betrayed millions of readers through his popular book that she had helped propel to the bestsellers lists. She pulled the book from Oprah's Book Club. Though I generally agree with Oprah, this is the one time I recall when I just did not agree with her. The message of the book touched me so deeply that, to me, it was irrelevant whether it was true or not. While some of the exact situations may not have happened to James Frey, circumstances such as these do happen to thousands of people every day. The message of the book remained true: Addiction is complex and can destroy lives for generations.

Frey provided vivid descriptions of cravings for alcohol or drugs. He showed how the most minor of circumstances could trigger a thought that would then trigger the desire. It was like having a permanent itch. You feel a strong desire to scratch it, but you have made that mistake before. You know that once you scratch it, it will only itch more intensely. Frey talks about trying to sit on his hands to keep from grabbing the bottle that he so desired. In his stream of consciousness style with its lack of punctuation, Frey helps the reader feel the state of confusion that characterizes the inner world of an addict. Sitting on his hands becomes harder as his feelings escalate to panic and self-destruction. He talks about the need to sit still, but as his hands shake beneath his body, you understand how grabbing it could win out.

Addicts become sober when they learn how to hold on through the triggers and the cravings. When they learn how to hold back rather than acting on emotion or the lack of it. When they learn to not allow the feeling to manipulate them and refuse to numb it out. Addicts achieve sobriety when they can feel and hold on anyway.

Eventually the urge will end. It will pass—because all things do. Nothing is permanent—not even an itch. I wasn't an addict, and other than my grandfather, I had not been affected firsthand by someone who was. But I remember connecting to the idea that whatever I go through, I can just hold on. There was such a relief for me in just knowing that it was okay to *not act*. To *do nothing*.

Throughout my life I had always thought I had to fix it, to figure it out. No matter what happened in my life, I never waited. I would gather information, make a decision, and get right on it—not wasting a second of time. Simply sitting in the mess and holding on felt silly to me. "Doing something" or taking immediate action was my own way of not dealing with the hurt and numbing my emotions. And I was good at it. But deep down at my core, it was also destroying me. The pressure associated with having to fix everything was massive.

Years after I read Frey's book, as I poured my heart, time, energy, and money into a man who struggled with addiction, I fell into the trap of trying to rescue him. That was my natural instinct. *I can fix this. I know how to fix this.* The problem is "this" is not a thing—it's a person. And people cannot be fixed by another person. People are "fixed" by their own desire, willpower, and determination. He was the only one who could save himself.

He went to treatment and one week I accompanied him for family planning at the treatment center. The counselor took us into a room and told us we were going to physically act out our relationship roles and how we react to each other. As we talked through our frustrations or desires, she had us get into a position that illustrated that thought. At one point, Travis was on the ground curled up in a ball looking at me, and I was in a running position hovering over him. This was my "rescuer" stance.

As we froze in that position, the counselor said, "Travis, she is running to help while you are struggling. How does that make you feel?" Without saying a word, he stayed curled in the ball and simply turned around and put his back to me. He wanted to struggle in isolation—away from me. The counselor asked me what outcome

I wanted. I sat down beside him and hugged him. He uncurled and hugged me back.

Sit. Stay. Hold on.

My natural instinct is to spring into action. That exercise reminded me of the importance of just sitting still. When we are healthy, we can sit in the thoughts, feelings, temptations, and struggles. We are strong enough to sit still and wait them out. The addict experiences a breakthrough when he learns to simply hold on and stand his ground against temptations and old patterns. Not taking action in moments of chaos and crisis is the healthiest course of action for both the addict and the rescuer. Sometimes, holding on is our only option.

I lived in Mississippi when Hurricane Katrina destroyed parts of the South. I volunteered to be on a first-response team that landed in the Mississippi Gulf Coast weeks after the devastation. I could not believe my eyes. I was standing in the middle of the destruction and I could not process how it happened and how anyone survived it. Several years later when I was working in junior college athletics, we had a quarterback join us who grew up in Louisiana. Randall Mackey had the most beautiful green eyes you have ever seen. And if you looked at them closely, you could see the trauma and pain. He was a Hurricane Katrina survivor. The town he lived in, Port Sulphur, Louisiana, was destroyed when the eye of the hurricane passed directly over it. Afterward it became a ghost town. Others had provided me with several accounts of how the young man had survived the storm. In one of them, he had been found floating in water on top of a car. In another account, he was at the school in the gym and swam out to save himself. I never asked him what the real truth was.

I do know that the actual hurricane was just the start of his trauma. His town was wiped out and he had to move to a new town and attend a new high school. He struggled even finding words after that. People told me he was mute. At one point he was found gripping a football and just rocking back and forth. He was just holding on. That was really all he could do. Nothing was in his control—not the storm, and not his ability to recover from it. He held on until he had an option to move and then he got up…and fought! He walked on the practice field at his new school and channeled all the emotion he'd been holding onto

With Randall Mackey, former EMCC and Ole Miss quarterback and Hurricane Katrina survivor.

into his sport. He led his team to multiple state championships, never losing a high school game. He was the Louisiana State High School Player of the Year his senior year. Sit. Stay. Move.

Know When It's Time to Take Action

Holding on is for a season. We eventually have to do *something*. We hold on through the thick of the emotions, temptations, and trauma, and then we move. The important thing is knowing which direction we should go. We must identify where to direct and channel the energy we've saved.

The Serenity Prayer states:

> God grant me the serenity to accept the things I cannot change, the courage to change the things I can, and the wisdom to know the difference.

There are things in life we simply cannot control and we must only focus on the things we can. The first thing they tell an addict's loved ones is "You didn't cause it, you can't cure it, and you can't control it." Most of the time there seems to be a lot more things in life we can't control than things we can. We can't control natural disasters, pandemics, cancer, or other tragedies. We also don't control when and how the next chance will show up in our lives. What we can control is our responses and the actions we take. We can hold on through it, seek clarity to cope in healthy ways, and then do the work to overcome our circumstances. We must understand the things we can control and let go of the things we can't.

Travis and I spent eight months apart after he was released from his treatment center. After being separated during this time, we decided to try our relationship again. I hoped his journey to recovery had been successful. I had also been at work unpacking and unraveling the trauma I had experienced in walking through addiction with someone I loved.

Once back together, we started working through the brokenness the addiction had caused in both of us. I quickly found myself back in the same spiral. Some things had changed, but a lot had stayed the same. I didn't trust him and he didn't feel safe. We blamed each other and clawed to be the one sitting in the victim seat. I found myself regularly triggered and apologizing for my own weaknesses—and resentful of his. After several weeks, I realized we were in the exact same unhealthy patterns we had fallen into before.

I struggled to accept this reality. I loved him, and I wanted our relationship to work. I had gone back into the relationship with this huge hope that he would be different and we would be different. I had a vision of the healthy relationship we could share. But that's where it ended—with a vision. The reality was he was not sober. I was not handling that well. We were not different. No matter what he said or what I wanted, we had to face the truth. I could not change it. I did not create it, and I could not control it. For five months I fought this reality. Eventually, I had to accept the things I couldn't change. Sit. Stay. Hold on. Accept.

Sometimes after we have accepted a really challenging reality, holding on looks a little different. We sit, stay, and when it comes time for the moving part—we move with a little more caution. Pain, disappointment, and trauma can act like an emotional handicap. Instead of lunging forward like an athlete in top condition, we move forward with a limp. After Travis and I had broken up, a friend wisely said, "If a person got sucker punched every time they walked out of their house, they would start to walk out slower." Now, when you open the front door to step out, you spend a minute surveying what is out there. You walk very cautiously to the end of the driveway. You earned that right. Trauma earns you the right to proceed with caution next time you walk out of the house.

When we have gone through trauma and finally learn to move again, we need to hold on—literally—to a support system. We need to grab the rails and put all our weight on them. We need to walk slowly and deliberately to trust that our legs will carry us. And sometimes we can't move at all and we just need to be carried.

We Can't Do Life Alone

I was scrolling through Twitter one day a few football seasons ago and I saw a video of a football team carrying a teammate up the steps to the top of the stadium. Their teammate had been injured in a game the year before and was paralyzed. He needed them and they needed him. They leaned on one another that day. From this lofty vantage point, he could see the view of that field he used to run onto again because he was carried by his teammates. We can't do life alone. At times, we simply don't have the strength or the ability, and we need to hold on to something or somebody else. We need to just be picked up and carried. Sit. Stay. Hold on. Support.

Whenever I think about this concept of holding on, I think about my grandmother. She contracted polio in 1916 at the age of two and remained crippled for the rest of her life. She often got left behind or left out completely because of her handicap. Despite that, she maintained a positive attitude and a sweet, kind demeanor. She was a fantastic listener and an even better cook. She may have been disabled, but she could whip up an incredible lemon meringue pie that made your mouth water. At holiday gatherings, she would often cook three meals a day, every day. We would crowd around her dining room table for each one. That table now sits in my own dining room.

Whenever a natural disaster or national crisis occurs, I think about Grandmama (as we all called her). I think about how scary it must have been for her parents—not knowing if she would live or what the quality of her life would look like. But with all the hardship she had to endure…SHE SURVIVED! She lived a long and wonderful life. She was married to the love of her life for sixty-six years, and gave birth to three healthy and wonderful children who grew up to be

even better adults. She lived to
know four grandchildren and
three great-grandchildren. She
played the piano beautifully
and graced us with her presence for ninety-one years. She
didn't just survive—she lived!

I never expected to experience a pandemic in my lifetime.
I thought those were reserved
for developing countries and
the "olden days." The year
2020 took us all by surprise
and forced us to sit. COVID-
19 demanded that we stop,
stay inside, and live differently than any of us ever imag-

My grandmother, Blanche Wagner, sitting at her
piano.

ined. Scary times—uncharted waters for us. Some of us have lived
through other tragic events—hurricanes, tornadoes, earthquakes, ter-
rorist attacks, and wars. And then there was the fear of impending
doom in the days leading up to Y2K when people around the world
panicked somewhat incessantly, thinking the new millennium would
mean the end of the world. But this felt different. We went through a
global health crisis—and life as we know it shutting down—in quarantine, unprecedented isolation, job loss. In other times of national
panic, we have risen to the occasion by coming together and helping
one another. We have gathered together and held hands and offered
comfort. This time, we were forced apart, disconnected, even from
our families, and left to fend for ourselves.

As a single mom, I was terrified of the unknowns. I was scared that my income would suffer and I wouldn't be able to provide for my daughter. I was fearful that navigating this alone with a child would be too much for me to handle. I was afraid of the loneliness and isolation being too much for my mental health to endure. While everyone else was complaining about being stuck in a house with their spouses, I was yearning for another adult with whom to spend these days. I had no one else to rely on. Everything was up to me. Though I had been in that situation before, I hadn't been isolated the way the coronavirus forced me to be. I had to be deliberate in what thoughts I allowed to enter my mind. I had to protect my own mental health and I also needed to protect my daughter's. I needed to remember and repeat the lesson that James Frey had taught me. This, too, shall pass, my friend. Just hold on.

Humans are social beings and people need connection. My hope for what comes after the holding-on phase of a pandemic is that, in disconnecting, we will be compelled to reconnect in a deeper, more genuine way. I hope we miss one another and crave to be connected. I hope we crave hugs and smiles and conversations rather than text messages, likes, and shares. I hope we come back stronger than ever and we crave real relationships and real intimacy rather than fake, superficial relationships fueled by false attention and a computer screen.

As challenging as uncertain times are, we are here to grow and learn from them. We are here to remember not only to survive—but to LIVE! The chances we receive in life—the experiences in which we succeed, and even those in which we fail—shape us. They make us into stronger people who are ready to take action when the time comes. As we learn to face reality, we can see more clearly that there are some things we can't control or change. No matter how badly we want to. There are times when the best and maybe only option we have is to hold on. To sit on our hands, cover our mouths, and just hold on. This, too, shall pass. Sit. Stay. Hold on. LIVE!

Sharpen Up!

Do nothing. Sometimes, the best course of action is to be still and allow the moment, the stress, the feeling, the craving to pass. In some situations, *not* acting is the action item.

Move. This, too, shall pass...and after it passes, get moving! Taking action immediately after holding on helps you avoid sinking back into negative patterns. Maybe that action is establishing an accountability partner, purging certain people or things from your life, or altering your daily plan to keep you on the right path. Then put one foot in front of the other and move forward.

Accept reality. Instead of listening to the fairy tales in your head or living in denial of the truth, look at what is actually happening in your life at *this* moment. What things can you control? What things can you change? Accept all the rest for a greater sense of peace.

Embrace support. Allow for others to help and support you, and offer them support in return. Human beings thrive off connection. We can't do life alone and we shouldn't have to. Find a support system and lean into it.

Live. Identify what makes you feel alive. For me, it's laughter, music, candles, fresh flowers, and the smell of the outdoors. For my grand-mama, it was offering a listening ear, cooking, and gathering her loved ones around the table. What makes you feel alive? Do those things! We are not in this world to just survive, we are here to *live*!

CHAPTER 8
Growth

"A mind that is stretched by a
new experience can never go back
to its old dimensions."

—OLIVER WENDELL HOLMES JR.

While I did not grow up in a rural area, I did grow up in Mississippi. While every state has dirt roads, the Deep South has more than most. We may not drive on them daily, and of course we also have paved interstates and highways. (We wear shoes, too!) But every Southern town has some dirt roads. When I was in high school, there wasn't a "night life" scene in my hometown, so we would go dirt-road ridin'. Dirt-road ridin' meant piling up in someone's truck and driving all the way down a long dirt road. On Friday nights, the guys would crank on the truck's deer lights and we would sit at the end of an old dirt road listening to music, talking, and drinking (Coke of course).

These dirt roads had ruts created by cars and trucks that had driven through mud that then hardened. Over time, the ruts would get deeper and deeper until no steering was needed. The truck's tires would just fall into the path already carved out. You could get the truck out of the ruts and onto a fresh patch of dirt, but the feat required horsepower and some heavy steering to accomplish.

Steering Along Our Neural Pathways

Our brains are a lot like those dirt roads. We have ruts in our brains —electrical patterns that form pathways over time. These ruts are our go-to reactions in situations, because we filter each new experience through prior experiences or trauma. We travel down these brain ruts with no steering and little intentional thought. Many times, we don't even know why we think this way or do these things. We just do. For example, maybe we self-sabotage at a certain spot in a new relationship. Perhaps we fly off the handle when we sense someone is disrespecting us. Or maybe we pop open a bottle or eat an extra piece of cake when we have had a hard day.

In order to change, we have to acknowledge the rut and take deliberate action to steer to a different path. That requires effort but it is possible to form a new rut in the road, a new path in our brain. Many studies have been conducted on *neuroplasticity*, the brain's ability to reorganize itself throughout a person's life. Our neural pathways change based on our environment, our thinking, and our emotions. The older we get, the more elusive real change can seem. You know the "you can't teach an old dog new tricks" principle? Science has an explanation for that. Research shows that our brain's default mode is to create well-worn paths of thinking, making us more set in our ways and bad attitudes over time. A 2018 *Forbes* article written by Tara

Swart, titled "The 4 Underlying Principles of Changing Your Brain," states:

> Neuroplasticity is the brain's ability to change itself constantly by creating new neural pathways and losing those which are no longer used. Encouraging the brain's neuroplasticity is the key to sustained adult learning and emotional intelligence, which will help the brain remain open-minded, intuitive and able to overcome biases throughout adulthood.

In fact, scientists stress that neuroplasticity is a key to a long and fulfilling life. As we encounter various situations, we can discipline ourselves to react in new ways. This amounts to grabbing the wheel and taking responsibility for the road we drive down. In order to be our absolute best self, we have to grow and create new pathways. It is neither easy nor fast, but it is possible.

A Change of Perspective Can Change Your Path

If we want where we're going to look significantly different than where we've been, personal growth is essential. In fact, difficult times push us toward growth. I think on some level we all want to do better. No one wakes up wanting to be a failure. Sometimes we just get stuck. Or maybe we were handed a bad situation to start. We may feel overwhelmed or simply not know what to do. We may be in denial that we need to do anything at all.

Have you ever watched someone do their job and think, *I could never do that*? There is a good chance someone would also look at you and say the same thing. Each person is born with an enormous amount of potential. But we're not born with the qualities we need to be great at *everything*. As adults, we play different roles in our lives and each requires different qualities. Some situations require greater patience, and others require less patience and more tenacity and grit. Our external and internal experiences impact the mixture and ratio of qualities we possess, and how they show up in different circumstances or roles.

I remember following the story of a professional tennis player and her quest for greatness. Physically, she was at the top of her game and could beat anyone. And she did—until she made it to the final rounds of a major tournament, when her ranking and championship money were on the line. Then she would choke. Every single time. She was so frustrated because she knew she was a top-notch athlete physically. Her struggle was entirely mental. She decided to see a sports psychologist, who asked her, "What is the quality you deem the most valuable in others?" Her answer: "Fairness."

In the name of "fairness," she often sabotaged her own success. She would be on the court beating an opponent, but then her mind would subconsciously tell her she wasn't being "fair" and she would lose the match. Once the psychologist figured this out, he worked with her to create an alter ego. As a human being, fairness was an admirable quality for her to exhibit. But as a professional tennis player, this quality hindered her competitiveness and ability to win. Her therapist asked her to make a list of the qualities she needed to be the best female tennis player in the world. She then worked on creating a separate persona that embraced and cultivated those qualities.

She developed a physical and mental routine before each tennis match. She recited mantras to herself while looking in the mirror, mantras about how powerful and strong she was. She would slip on wristbands as part of this routine, with similar words and messages inscribed on them. Every piece of equipment, and everything in her space before a tennis match reminded her of her new alter ego. The woman no longer elevated a sense of fairness over winning. On the court, she became a different person with a different mindset, which allowed her to excel in her career.

Don't Hit the Default Button

We all have places in our lives where we need to diverge from our default habits or behaviors. We may even have a role in our life where we need to create different pathways to succeed. For example, the word used most often to describe me, by both *Last Chance U* fans and the media, is "patient." That is *not* a word most of my friends would use to describe me. Before I became a mother, I felt like the least patient person on the planet. I wanted things done *now* and my way. After having my daughter, Kennedy, I changed. You would have thought I'd sipped on a magical elixir that filled me with forbearance.

A few years into working with junior college athletes, however, I felt like I had hit a wall. My attitude stank and I felt my effectiveness slipping. I began examining my habits and ruts to discover what I needed to do differently. The story of the tennis player I mentioned came to my mind. So, I made a list of the ten most important qualities I thought the best athletic academic counselor in the world should possess. The quality at the top of that list: patience. Oh no! I was lacking that quality as a counselor. I only had it as a mom—sometimes. I looked at my list and decided I *could* develop patience and all the other qualities I needed to be the best counselor possible.

For a long time, I focused on just being more patient. First, I changed my routine. Driving to work each day, I would spend ten minutes listening to calming meditations. As I walked across the threshold to my office, I'd say to myself, *I am the most patient, understanding, kind, compassionate athletic academic counselor in the world. I am good at this.* I was changing the pathways in my brain in regard to who I believed I was as an academic counselor. Patience and tranquility did not come to me naturally, but they were the characteristics I needed to sustain the right energy and mindset for my job. I had the power to change.

My new routine prepared me for the belligerent student who didn't want to hear what I had to say. It equipped me to deal with the demanding coach breathing down my neck for answers on why a star athlete was failing his classes. It steeled me for coworkers questioning or even criticizing my methods. Whatever the stress, I knew I could take three deep breaths before responding and be patient Brittany. Later, as I watched myself on Netflix, I could see how my efforts had paid off. I was patient—both as a mom and as a counselor.

Here is the key to growth: We must recognize we need it! Growth does not just happen. Those grooves will just keep getting deeper as we live life on autopilot. Until we're willing to admit that we are contributing to the problem, we won't be motivated to take the steps necessary to change or do something differently. And we won't recognize the need to steer out of the ruts unless we show up for our own lives. Every single day is an opportunity for growth, but only if we are actively living the days!

Like that tennis player, you have to get real with yourself and the emotions you're experiencing. Suppressing feelings never leads to growth. You must use your honest feelings and observations—"I'm not a patient academic counselor"—and channel them into something productive—"Here are three things I can do today to be more patient."

While I wasn't born patient, I'm an extremely passionate person. I am intense and I know it. I wouldn't say I'm an angry person, but I definitely experience anger. For a long time, I did not feel anger was an acceptable emotion for me. It wasn't ladylike. The societal norms of a good Southern woman being meek and quiet got the best of me at times. After a situation where my passion and inner drive had been apparent, I would become my own internal critic, feeling like I'd done something wrong. *Why can't I just be quiet like a good Southern woman is supposed to be?* I would beat myself up for feeling angry or being "intense."

One day I walked into a boxing gym. I had seen it on social media, but I have no idea why I actually walked inside. I loved the yoga studio and people where I practiced in Meridian, Mississippi. After moving to Alabama, I just could not find the same experience with a yoga studio so I gave it up. Maybe that is why I walked in the boxing gym that day. I was searching for the internal and external transformation similar to what yoga had been for me in Mississippi. The reason for entering didn't change the fact that I had never hit anything in my life. I honestly think if a person sucker punched me, I would literally turn the other cheek. This particular spot, Battle Republic in Birmingham, Alabama, was a glove-up, fight-on, all-out boxing gym. Each client had his or her own bag, with twenty-two bags in the space. The setting was dark, with only neon LED lights glowing, and loud! My first time, a coach walked in and quickly taught me the six punches. For the next forty-five minutes she yelled punch combinations while the music blared and I hit my own water-filled punching bags.

I returned again and again. Some days, tears streamed down my face as I released thirty-plus years of anger on bag number seven. I saw faces of people who'd hurt me in that bag. I saw words of negative self-talk I'd repeated to myself for decades. Through boxing, I allowed myself to feel the negative emotions I needed to feel and unleash the anger and hurt. For me, boxing allowed me to channel those feelings into a healthy outlet. For others, that activity may be running, painting, singing, writing, dancing, yoga, or gardening. But we all need an outlet to release these emotions in a healthy way.

At my home boxing gym, Battle Republic.

© Kristopher Noah

Be Proactive, Not Reactive

In football, the defensive line position requires a ruthless pursuit and attack. While the offensive lineman's job is to protect the quarterback by creating a safe pocket for him to play in, the defensive lineman's job is to destroy that pocket during every single play. After working with college football players for a while, I realized that the ones who played defense were usually the hardest guys to deal with off the field. Defensive linemen are big people who often possess big tempers. Surprisingly, they were my favorite student-athletes to work with. But they were challenging. Many of them had troubled pasts, and I could see the pain in their eyes. Some struggled with managing their anger and controlling aggressive behavior off the field. If we could get past all the crap, I knew I would find an amazingly sweet soul behind it. The guys who worked through their issues were usually relentless on the field. They unleashed every bit of the pain and anger when they lined up across from their opponents every Saturday. I would be shocked sometimes at just how "mean" they could become once they put that uniform on. Years later, as I slid my boxing gloves on, ready to unleash my inner beast, I understood the power of channeling negative energy into something productive.

New York Times bestselling author Michael Singer says, "You are causing the vast majority of your own problems due to your mental reactions. You have the right to choose not to do that." Growth means being *proactive* rather than *reactive*. When you're experiencing inner turmoil, it's hard to keep a clear head and make the right decisions. The good news is, you don't have to. Until we get to a place where we are able to make solid decisions in the middle of a stressful situation or crisis, we can work toward that by choosing to be proactive.

I talked to defensive linemen about how they could be proactive even when they were overcome with anger on the field. They described how once the adrenaline was flowing and the heart was pounding and their thoughts were swirling, it was essential to stay connected to their purpose and the game plan. A fifteen-yard penalty for unsportsmanlike conduct counteracted the purpose and the plan. The overall game plan was bigger than this one moment. And so they trained themselves to never get to a heightened state of emotion that could jeopardize the point of them being on the field.

I taught them to apply these same principles to the classroom. "If you're in class and you feel yourself getting worked up, politely and quietly get up and walk out," I would tell them. "Remove yourself from the situation before you react to the negative feeling." This sometimes happened to the athletes because they felt uncomfortable, not "enough," and acted out as a defense mechanism. Different guys had different routines to calm themselves. Some would go for a walk around the building. Others would go sit in the bathroom stall and breathe. Still others would come into my office, slam the door, and talk it out. Once the student had calmed down and was in a different state of mind, he could return to the classroom and handle the situation appropriately. Each player had a plan for how to ride out those difficult moments without losing his cool.

Not everyone experiences anger issues. Sometimes the trigger is stress. As a single mom, I felt extremely stressed when I came home after a long day at work. I had a forty-mile daily commute to and from work. I would pick up my daughter, Kennedy, from the Boys & Girls Club around 5 PM, feeling super guilty that she had been there since 7:30 AM. I was tired, my feet hurt, and I would walk into my house and immediately be overwhelmed by the weight of everything I still needed to get done.

In a session one day, my therapist said, "How can we eliminate that negative feeling you experience right when you walk in the door? What can you change to feel relaxed and comfortable rather than anxious?" That's when I realized an unlikely culprit of my stress. I realized that when I opened the door from the garage into my house each day, the first thing I saw was my bedroom. The unmade bed that met my gaze stressed me out. It reminded me of my hectic morning. It made me feel out of control and like my entire house was a mess (which wasn't the case). My therapist instructed me to change my morning routine and allow myself an extra ten minutes to clean up the area that I would see as I walked in the door at 5:15 each evening.

I have made my bed every single day since then. No matter what. There was something about walking into my house and seeing my neatly made bed that immediately calmed and soothed me. What "bed" do you need to make to proactively set yourself up for a different reaction? Maybe you need to sit in the car in the driveway for ten minutes to prepare yourself for your children or a big meeting. Maybe you need to schedule one day to pay all the bills so you aren't stressed out about finances every day. Maybe you need to change the lighting or scent of your space to create a more positive vibe.

Perhaps, like the defensive linemen I worked with, you need to create a plan for steering clear of triggers. Maybe you need a plan for how to remove yourself from environments, conversations, or activities that do not feel safe. Thinking through what might throw us off our game, and mitigating potential damages, leads to growth. A proactive plan to minimize the effect stressors have on our lives helps us change our mindset and habits. We won't always need to be so proactive. Each of us is evolving and working toward changing the ruts and pathways of our brains. But in the meantime—even a single step forward is growth.

No matter our background or current role in life, each of us is responsible for our own actions, momentum, and growth. Recently, as I was scrolling through social media, I came upon a picture of a sign posted on the front doors of a hospital in Indiana. Usually a sign would not catch my eye, but this one did. Here's the message that made me take notice:

> Please take responsibility for the energy you bring into this space. Your words matter. Your behaviors matter. Our patients and our teams matter. Take a slow, deep breath and make sure your energy is in check before entering. Thank you.

We are responsible for the energy and attitude we bring into every situation. We control what we add to, or take away from, a space and the people in that space. I wish I had learned the power of my vibe a long time ago. I entered many meetings during my time in education that were dull and lifeless. I allowed others' behavior to suck the life out of my own. I wish I could walk back into some of those meetings as the person I am now, knowing my value and bringing confidence that my opinions, and those of others in the room, matter. I wonder if the outcomes of those meetings would have been different. Maybe we would have actually solved problems rather than trying to just speed the meeting up to escape the gloom and misery of everyone around us.

We matter. Our words, behaviors, and attitudes matter. We can fill others with confidence or we can kill it. We can offer them a safe space of encouragement and hope, or we can fill them with fear of what will happen when they fail. We can be a part of the solution in their lives or contribute to the problems. We can be intentional about getting out of ruts and steering toward growth in our own lives and then help others do the same.

Sharpen Up!

Make a list. Write down the qualities needed to be most effective in the role you are trying to succeed at (personal or career). Circle the qualities you are already strong in. Notice the ones you need to enhance or develop. Choose one quality at a time to focus on. Now write out three strategies that you can implement to help develop this quality. For instance:

Quality: Patience

• I will take three big deep breaths before responding to someone.

- I will squeeze a stress ball under my desk during hard conversations to help me focus on what I am saying and who I want to be in that moment.

- I will take a walk or go for a short drive to hit the reset button either after a difficult situation or conversation or in anticipation of one in order to stop myself from creating a worse outcome than is necessary.

Speak positive affirmations. When we speak our desires, our brain follows. Did you know that when you smile, even if it's fake, your brain signals that you're happy? There is a powerful connection between what we say and what becomes reality. So speak growth into existence. Write the following words on your mirror or a sticky note placed where you will see it daily:

"I am _____

_____."

Say the statement to yourself over and over throughout your day.

Channel your emotions. Suppressing or denying negative emotions forms a barrier to growth. Allow yourself to feel painful emotions. Then channel those feelings into a productive avenue. The athletes I worked with had football. I have boxing. Find your own activity that allows you to release stress, anger, and anxiety so you can get moving toward growth.

Be proactive. I've said it before and I'll say it again: Have a plan. Having a plan is half the battle. Don't wait until you are engulfed in flames to come up with a fire escape plan. Think ahead about ways your growth may be hindered, and decide what you will do and how you will react if this happens. What are emotions you may experience that trigger you to slip back into your ruts? What can you do to diminish these triggering emotions?

For example, stress affects patience. When I am stressed, I become less patient. So how can I diminish stressful situations and set myself up for growing into a more patient person? For me, focusing on what I have accomplished, rather than what I still have left to accomplish, helps me to eliminate stress. I will stop myself from the stress reactions and mentally remind myself of what I have gotten accomplished today. Or sometimes, I stop and make a to-do list just so I can cross the things I have already done off it. This allows my brain to calm down, my heart rate to slow, and stress levels to lower, and it gives me a moment to think about a proper response rather than speaking garbage that not only damages trust but also sidetracks me from developing the quality of patience.

CHAPTER 9
Be the Solution

"In order to be proud of yourself, you have
to do things you are proud of."

-UNKNOWN

I sat in the head football coach's office at a high school in Baltimore. One at a time, the players filed in to meet me. The school had hired me as a consultant to help them serve their athletes better, and the players just wanted to meet "the lady from *Last Chance U.*" I was equally excited to meet them!

"I can't wait for you to meet this next guy," the coach said, his eyes lighting up.

A solid-looking linebacker walked in, looked me square in the eye, introduced himself, and shook my hand. After the young man left, Coach filled me in on his story. The young man had turned up in the coach's office one day, escorted by police officers, and wearing a T-shirt emblazoned with the logo of the school's football team. The kid didn't say a word, so the police officer offered an explanation. "We found this kid sleeping in the laundromat. He can't sleep there. He won't talk to us, but we assumed he played football here because of his shirt. Maybe you can find him a different place to sleep."

The teenager didn't play football at that high school. In fact, the coach had never seen him before. After the police left, Coach sat him down to hear his story. The kid apologized—he didn't mean to cause any trouble. He explained that he'd found the T-shirt in a dumpster. He became homeless after he and his mom had been evicted from their apartment. His mother was an addict and unable to care for him, so he'd been living on his own ever since. He'd been bouncing around from place to place, which had made it difficult for him to stay in school and play football, so he'd dropped out. Hearing about his struggles, Coach decided to help. He offered him a chance to earn a spot on his football team and didn't stop there. He knew this kid needed safety and stability, and that was bigger than being on a team. The coach offered him a bed in a row house the school owned to provide shelter to other kids just like him. (The school owns several of these houses for students in this situation, and an assistant coach lives with the students.) He gave him a school uniform, books, and a tutor.

This young man, who had walked into that high school in a crisis, went on to earn a college scholarship. He started out with a 1.75 GPA. A year later, he'd achieved a 3.5 GPA. Solutions change lives! That young man is a testament to that.

Meet People Where They Are

A big part of our own evolution and growth as human beings is becoming a positive influence on others. As we pursue our own next chance, it is important to look for ways to help others find that as well. Helping others find solutions is not only rewarding, it also leads to the kind of overall connection in a community that stirs up more opportunities. Not to mention, there's a lot to learn from those you help along the way.

Being a part of the solution for others requires us to meet people where they are. When I was a little girl, my dad taught me a valuable lesson. He said that some people are born on third base but think they hit a triple. In other words, some of us are born in a position of privilege that automatically gives us a leg up in the game of life. Others are born into less ideal circumstances. I was born in Mississippi! I'll tell you more about how that affected me in the next chapter. But let's say that label and the misconceptions about it didn't do me any favors. Going back to the baseball analogy, it's like some of us start out on first base, others on second, and still others on third. Maybe some of us aren't even on base yet! Wherever we start is neither a credit nor a shame to us. It simply is what it is. For those of us fortunate enough to start on third, though, it's important to understand that *we* didn't hit the triple. We didn't earn that spot. We were *given* a head start.

Some people may not even be on the field yet. They are fighting for a spot in the dugout. It's not their fault; it's their reality. They may not come from privilege, but they have the same dreams. Being a part of the solution means taking ownership of our own "starting spot" and also recognizing and accepting the starting spot of others. We must think responsibly about how we can equalize the playing field. We—as a neighborhood, as a community, as a corporation, as a state, as a country, as a human race—are only as good as the weakest link. There is enough for everyone. We rise collectively when each individual is allowed and encouraged to rise. We rise collectively when we are all seen and treated as equals.

Eric Jensen explores this very issue in his book *Teaching with Poverty in Mind*. A concept he addresses, which I love, is that if you aren't getting the reaction you expect, assume you need to teach it. Before I became an academic counselor at EMCC, I know what I assumed. I assumed that if I wasn't getting the reaction I expected from students, then something was wrong with them. Because nothing could be wrong with me or my expectations. Right?

I still had a lot to learn.

If we follow the philosophy of teaching and modeling behavior to young children so they can learn how to navigate the world, why do we balk at this philosophy when it comes to students who are older? Too often, we embrace teaching tools for students only until a certain age. If students haven't received the lesson by the cutoff, we start punishing them for it.

Solution-based thinking requires us to stop punishing, and instead identify the desired expectation and figure out how to teach what is not known. The alternative is like throwing a five-year-old in a kindergarten class and expecting him to read the rules. Let's use the example of our basic expectation of how someone will behave while eating out. We expect the person to show up dressed appropriately. We expect him to place the napkin on his lap. We expect him to know how to order off a menu and to not slurp the spaghetti noodles. However, if a person has never eaten in a quiet, nice restaurant, how are they supposed to know the proper etiquette?

There are football programs that provide their players with etiquette classes where they teach them which fork to use and other "table manners" for dining in a formal setting. Many of these young men have never had two forks to choose between, so they have no idea how to meet the expectation in a white tablecloth environment.

Not knowing is not the same as not wanting to know. We can teach the desired behavior.

To be a part of the solution, we have to discard the labels people and society place on us. We have to stop believing the hype when people say what we can and cannot do. What would happen if we let go of the labels and just let ourselves and others *be*? Let them achieve? I love a quote by thirty-two-year-old rapper Prince Ea, who captures this labeling issue perfectly. He essentially directs us to quit checking boxes—the boxes of fake labels that we then live down to. Labels that convince us to be small and trapped in a box, afraid to freely act as ourselves and live to the largeness that we are capable of. Those same boxes blur our vision when we attempt to see others and care for them. We use the artificial labels against others in the same way that we limit ourselves.

Don't Limit Yourself or Others with Labels

The problem is that we love labels. But labels can be limiting. In season two of *Last Chance U*, one of my student-athletes, Tim Bonner, bounced onto the scene. I say "bounced" because he is one of the most high-energy people I have ever met. That guy is *a lot*! He's always smiling, always laughing, always energetic. He introduced himself to me by saying, "My name is Tim Bonner, and I can only take A/B tests."

I had no idea what Tim was talking about. I had been an athletic academic counselor for over ten years but had no clue what an "A/B test" was. I looked at him quizzically and said something like: "Hi, Tim. Nice to meet you. What are you talking about?"

He repeated, "I can only take A/B tests." Then he explained, "When I was in elementary school, they told me I wasn't smart enough to choose from four choices; I could only choose between two." A

On the field at Florida Atlantic University with Tim Bonner.

lightbulb went off in my head. That belittling remark had become his identity. That label someone else had assigned to him had become so ingrained in his mind that he included it when he arrived at college and introduced himself to me. My heart sank.

I told Tim someone had lied to him in elementary school and he was most definitely smart enough to choose between four choices. He would take the same test everyone else took, and he would be just fine.

And that's what he did. Tim Bonner graduated from Florida Atlantic University after making the Dean's Honors List several times and being named Student Athlete of the Week.

I am not discounting real learning disabilities. My mom was a special education teacher, and I have seen the struggles of students who have had to manage learning differences. I applaud the teachers who provide them with needed support to succeed. However, in some cases we hinder students by slapping labels on them and then expecting less of them. Labels affect our mindset. We start to believe a label and allow it to change how we function, how we see ourselves, and ultimately affect the person we become. We allow an ACT score to tell us what college we can go to; our sex to tell us what position or paycheck we can aspire to; a bank account to tell us if we deserve to have our basic needs met. If we stop checking boxes and stop letting society define who we can become, our potential is boundless.

I recently started a new job as an adjunct college professor at a four-year university in Alabama. I'm passionate about college students and thrilled to be back on a college campus. Every Tuesday and Thursday, I am filled with energy when my students walk into my classroom. I get there early because my favorite part is the fifteen minutes or so before class starts when my students and I can just talk. I ask them questions and they openly engage in conversation with me. I love it. My expectation is that every professor should love this engagement and love the students. Otherwise, why teach?

In my days as an advisor, students would come to tell me that their professors had locked them out of class. They were trying to "teach" their students to be on time, so they would lock the door at 8:01 AM and not allow students who were running late to enter. I understand these professors' strategy, but I do not think it is an effective one for being a part of the solution. The goal is to educate, and students cannot be educated if we are not allowing them to enter the classroom. Being a part of the solution means having policies that are effectively serving the clientele. I have often wondered how these professors would feel if the doctor's office wouldn't allow them to enter when they showed up for an appointment a minute late. It doesn't align with the end goal. A doctor needs to see patients in order to heal them. A teacher needs to see students in order to educate them. Locking people out defeats the purpose. We cannot be part of the solution if our policies are punitive rather than constructive.

My child has the same awareness and concern for others that I do. In the second grade, Kennedy had a friend, Lacey, who was one of seven children to a single mom who worked multiple jobs. Kennedy loved Lacey. They sat by each other every day in the cafeteria and played on the playground together. The teacher even contacted me to tell me how special their friendship was. I knew Lacey's situation and would send extra money to pay for her class field trips or a snack on some days. I sent extra uniforms to the school counselor because Kennedy noticed a food stain was on Lacey's shirt multiple days in a row. I could imagine her mom's struggle to just keep it together. It had to be hard.

One winter day, Kennedy came home very upset because Lacey had been sent to the principal's office. When she calmed down enough to tell me the story, she said, "Mom, she had a pink coat on." What? She got sent to the principal's office because of a pink coat?

The school dress code policy stated that outerwear had to fit within the guidelines of the dress code. That meant that coats had to be plain red, white, or gray. The school board had decided that enforcing this policy was important, so any child who did not adhere would be pulled from class and sent home. Lacey had a pink coat. She was sent home.

Kennedy was devastated that her school—a place meant to be safe—had punished her friend for something so trivial, and I was irate. I called the school and asked them to show me the research that proved kids in a pink coat learned less than kids in a gray coat. I asked them not to send another student home because of the color of their coat or I would contact the local media. Lacey was safe—for now.

We lived in Mississippi, the poorest state in our country. My child attended a public school in a county where, according to the US Census, the median household income was $41,704. I suspected that Lacey's mom either jeopardized or lost her minimum-wage job that day when she had to abruptly leave work to pick her daughter up from school. I also suspected that Lacey was super proud of that pink coat after excitedly picking it out at the local secondhand store.

To pull a child out of class because of what they are wearing is traumatizing and embarrassing for that student. I have seen firsthand the long-term effects of that type of educational embarrassment play out in a college classroom. How do we expect Lacey to be excited about learning and showing up at school when we single her out because of her family's income level? This is not solution-based thinking. We aren't all born on third base.

I could also call this "sweating the small stuff." Being a part of real, long-term, life-changing solutions means we can't sweat the small stuff. Small stuff is a short-term problem, and getting caught up in it hinders life-changing work from being done. I wrote in Chapter 4 about Ronald Ollie and his headphones. My worrying about and throwing a temper tantrum over his headphones would have been a sweat-the-small-stuff reaction. The bigger goal was to develop a trusting relationship with a student who needed a positive, safe support system. The solution was bigger than a pair of headphones.

Don't Limit Future Greatness with Minutia and Rigidity

Educational policies and guidelines are often created with good intentions in mind. The trouble arises, however, when we want to fill in the gaps with small details and protocols to satisfy our own agenda. We start to get too nitpicky. It is at this stage, in my opinion, that we should default to being human. Rather than spelling out all the scenarios and all the details, we need to leave some space for people to make mistakes. We need to make space for second, and third, and fourth chances.

We can solve problems when we accept each student for who they are and where they are in this moment. We can solve problems when we treat them as individuals rather than make assumptions or generalizations about them and where they're coming from. We can solve problems when we approach with common sense and the ability to think open-mindedly. In solution-based thinking, everyone isn't treated the same. The same rules don't apply to all our students, and that's okay. I'll say it one more time: We aren't all born on third base.

Nick Saban, arguably the best coach in college football history, made the hour and a half trip from Tuscaloosa to Scooba a few times while I worked at EMCC. He is a man small in stature but intimidating nonetheless: He's all business and no small talk. He once referred to me as the "best coach EMCC had." I was incredibly flattered by that compliment. Coach Saban doesn't know it, but he changed my life in a big way long before I met him.

He was the head coach at Michigan State University, and during his time there, he had an offensive player who found himself in some deep trouble. Everyone wanted Coach Saban to get rid of this player, and he had been taking the heat on this issue for days. When it came time for his weekly press conference, a reporter asked him about his decision not to kick Muhsin Muhammad off the team. Coach Saban paused and then asked the room, "What is the alternative? You want him gone? You realize in doing that you are removing him from a structured environment, with a place to live and hope for a future. You want him back on the streets to end up in prison or dead."

What he said next impacted me forever: "We are either part of the solution in this kid's life or we are part of the problem. But we can't be both."

Years later, another Alabama player coached by Nick Saban found himself in trouble. This time the decision was out of the coach's hands. The University of Alabama kicked DJ Pettway out of school and gave him a list of conditions he would have to meet before he could return to the university and its football program. Coach Saban sent DJ to me and the coaching staff at EMCC with the faith that DJ could earn back his spot playing for the Crimson Tide. As fate would have it, I'd watched the press conference at Michigan State and decided before I met DJ that I wanted to help him. I was now getting that chance while Saban, who had taught me how to be a part of the solution, looked on.

In 2014, Nick Saban held another press conference after DJ Pettway had returned to Alabama and helped the Crimson Tide win another national title. Asked about his decision to allow DJ back into his program, Coach Saban said:

> There's always a lot of criticism out there when somebody does something wrong. Everybody wants to know, "How are you going to punish the guy?" But there's not enough—for the nineteen-and twenty-year-old kids—people out there saying, "Why don't you give them another chance?" Where do you want them to be? I feel strong about this now, really strong about all the criticism for a guy who makes a mistake. My question to you is: Where do you want them to be? Condemned to a life sentence or have his children go to Princeton?

Muhsin Muhammad played fifteen years in the NFL and won the Carolina Panthers Man of the Year Award in 1999. He created a charity and now runs an investment firm. His daughter graduated from Princeton. DJ Pettway graduated from Alabama, played for the New Orleans Saints, and is now a coach and raising a son.

In our own lives and in the lives of others, we are either a part of the solution or part of the problem. Being a part of the solution is not always easy. It is a lot less time-consuming to silently contribute to the problem. Solution-based thinking requires careful thought. Martin Luther King Jr. said it best: "Rarely do we find men who will-

ingly engage in hard, solid thinking. There is an almost universal quest for easy answers and half-baked solutions. Nothing pains some people more than having to think."

I like to say being a part of the solution requires us to earn our paycheck. Being a part of the solution requires us to go the extra mile. It's the part of our job description that is not listed. It's also the part that creates real change.

We can beat someone up for coming to class without a pencil, or we can just hand them one. Being a part of the solution, and having grace for one

With DJ Pettway, who earned his way back to the University of Alabama.

another, is as important in our own second chances as it is in the lives of others. The action of being a part of the solution in someone else's life is like the final exam for our own growth. It demonstrates that we have evolved and are confident enough to pour our support and resources into someone else. That is the beauty of growth, change, and next chances. The true reward is passing it on. Once we've had an opportunity at our own second chances, we can help those that may not have the same resources. When we can meet an individual where they are and see past the restrictions placed on them, we give them their best chance at success and allow ourselves the greatest opportunity to help them in a truly meaningful way.

Sharpen up!

Meet people where they are. Meeting people where they are helps everyone. Unmet expectations create stress. If we go into a relationship ready to "start" at a certain spot, we set ourselves up for disappointment and stress when that expectation is not met. Allow people to show up and tell you who they are and then meet them right there. If a student reads at a fourth-grade level, you can't hand them a novel and expect them to comprehend it.

This is why I was reading English literature stories out loud to a room full of college students on *Last Chance U.* I knew in order for them to comprehend and remember the details of the literature, we would need to read a paragraph or two at a time and discuss what had been read. We would need to explore and talk about deeper meanings and character traits. We aren't all literature scholars and some haven't mastered reading comprehension tactics. I would be more effective (and less disappointed) just meeting these students exactly where they are.

Teach the reaction you expect. This might sound cliché but we know what we know. Whether an employee, a student, a coworker, or a child, if someone is behaving in a way that is not acceptable, start by exhibiting grace and patience. Then teach (either by words or by example) a more acceptable solution. Not long ago, I was providing consulting for a youth organization in Belle Glade, Florida. During a closed-door meeting with the directors of this center, students kept interrupting us. I realized an expectation was not being met because the students didn't understand the expectation: Don't walk in on closed-door meetings. I stopped the meeting and taught the next student the expectation of knocking on the door, asking to interrupt, and then greeting the room. It took five tries for him to get it right, but he learned the acceptable reaction to a closed-door meeting that day.

Release the labels. Labels tend to put us and others in a box. As you interact with others, try to approach those situations with an open mind. Instead of making assumptions, ask questions and listen to get a fuller picture of what's going on. Allow others to show up as themselves rather than who you expect them to be based on labels.

Create solutions that effectively serve your constituents. "But it's the way we have always done it!" may be the *most* ineffective statement in business and in life. Ask and examine procedures and policies. Why do we do it this way? What does this policy achieve? Have things changed to make this way of doing things ineffective? Is it meaningful, beneficial, and honest? If a policy has become corrupt or ineffective, get rid of it.

Don't sweat the small stuff. In much of life, the little things matter because they add up to impact the big things. However, when it comes to building relationships, sweating the small stuff can be disastrous. No one likes a nag. Let the small stuff remain small and spend your energy finding solutions for the bigger issues.

CHAPTER 10
Dream Big

"No matter where you are from, your dreams are valid."
—LUPITA NYONG'O

When I graduated from Mississippi State, I wanted to work for ESPN. That was until I found out it was headquartered in Connecticut. *Girl, you can't make it in Connecticut,* I told myself. I was in my early twenties and didn't have the maturity to fully think this through. Connecticut was cold and far from my family. So instead of pursuing my dream, I chickened out. Somewhere rooted deep inside, I believed that I was just a Mississippi girl and needed to keep my dreams small.

Big dreams seemed frivolous and unattainable. I needed to be realistic. After all, I was just a girl from a small town. The great state of Mississippi has produced some incredibly successful and talented people: Oprah Winfrey, Brett Favre, Faith Hill, John Grisham, BB King, Tennessee Williams, James Earl Jones, and Elvis, to name but a few. Yet it's also the state that regularly finds itself at the bottom of the list. Mississippi is ranked the poorest state in the country, and its population is arguably one of the least educated and least physically healthy. Some would even say it's the state that offers its citizens the least amount of hope and opportunity.

These statistics, along with the state's less-than-glowing reputation, were hard for me to ignore as a child. In my own opinion, I was "good enough" for Mississippi, but not for anywhere else. I had big dreams, but who was I to think I could fly higher than the station I was born into?

To prepare for my college applications, I took the ACT test one time. I scored a 21, which is slightly better than the average score of 20.8, but not competitive. I scored so low on the math portion of the test that I would have to take intermediate algebra before I could enroll in a college-level algebra class. I had no idea what I wanted to do with my life, and I doubted I was smart enough for college. I let a test score, along with my B-student status, steal my confidence in my academic abilities.

Still, I wanted out of Mississippi. *If I can just get out of here, I can do better,* I thought. During my junior year of high school, my parents took me to visit the colleges on my dream list: Florida State, Auburn, Alabama, and virtually, through pictures from a friend I was planning on rooming with, UCLA. I remember stepping onto the campus of Florida State University. Within minutes, the panic set in. The campus was huge, with a mind-blowing number of students, philosophies, and beliefs. *I will get eaten alive here!* I thought. I felt the same sense of fear and doubt when I visited the other campuses on my list. I ended up squashing my big dream to attend one of my dream schools and instead settled for Mississippi State University.

When I look back on it now, it's ironic that the state I wanted to get out of so badly was the very place where my dreams came true. The not-so-shiny opportunity to be the athletic academic counselor at a tiny junior college in a town in Mississippi with a population barely over 700 people led me to appear on Netflix's *Last Chance U.* This wildly successful documentary series created a platform that enabled me to become a motivational speaker and start my own company. The

With my parents, Buddy Wagner and Brenda Dosher, and my daughter, Kennedy, after my induction into the Clinton Walk of Honor in my hometown of Clinton, Mississippi.

experience taught me not to let the labels that have been slapped on my life, including those of my own making, keep me from dreaming, believing, and achieving. No circumstance or experience is wasted. Each one, good or bad, can propel you to your greatest potential and allow you to seize opportunities when they come your way.

The Art of Dreaming Big

What are the restrictions you have put on your own dreams? What is society telling you about the likelihood that hopes will become reality? How can you break the binds of those limitations and find the confidence in yourself and your abilities to go for it? Let's explore the art of dreaming big!

The first important thing to consider is that not all big dreams become reality—at least not in the exact way you imagined. But that doesn't mean you should give up on your goal. If you have ever watched a college sporting event, you have seen the NCAA commercial that shows the college athletes excelling at something besides sports. The commercial ends with the statement, "The majority of our athletes will go pro in something other than sports." This is a true statement. The NCAA publishes a chart on its website every year that tallies the percentage of high school athletes who are talented enough to play in college, and then the percentage of college athletes who are talented enough to go pro. The numbers are staggeringly small. Going pro is every college athlete's dream. But only 1 percent of college football players will make an NFL roster.

I used to have this chart hanging in my office. We can't all go pro, and I wanted to stress to my athletes the importance of an education and earning a degree. Then one day a defensive lineman stood before me, refusing to put maximum effort into his academic work. He just didn't see the point. In his mind, he was going to play professional football. I told him to look at the chart and tell me what percentage of college football players go pro.

"One percent," he said.

"What does that tell you, Quinton?" I asked.

"That I have to be the one percent!"

I admired the young man's tenacity. He made an important point. Placing in the top 1 percent of anything is a very lofty goal. But if everyone allowed that statistic to squash their resolve, the number would be zero. In order to succeed in tough statistics, we need the unwavering confidence and belief that we can do it.

I couldn't argue that day with Quinton's confidence and determination. I would have to find a different avenue to persuade him that earning an education was just as important as also landing in that 1 percent. A piece of that was persuading him that he could be an athlete AND more. So far 100 percent of the professional football players I have worked with also earned a college degree.

Dream Big and Work Hard

As you consider the odds of your big dream happening, believe you *are* the 1 percent! Somebody has to be! I like to say, "Dream big. Work bigger." No matter how big or small your goals are, a strong work ethic will only help you. I credit my strong work ethic with leading me to a dream I didn't even know I had. I have always worked hard. I didn't always dream big, but I have always worked big. I've been called a lot of things, but lazy is not one of them.

Mary Barra, the first female CEO of General Motors, has also never been called lazy. She started at the bottom rung of the company ladder when she was an eighteen-year-old without a college degree.

According to a 2016 article in *Business Insider*, Barra climbed her way to the top because she was willing to work hard. Her colleagues reported that she was often the first person to arrive at the office in the morning and the last to leave at night.

I don't know about you, but stories of hard work paying off inspire me more than those that begin, "At five years old, I knew I wanted to be…" At five years old, I just wanted a stuffed animal and some ice cream. I didn't have a dream. Hell, at twenty, I didn't have a dream. But I sure as hell had a work ethic.

The stories of hard work paying off make me feel empowered and give me hope. A work ethic is something I can control. I'm in charge of how much effort I choose to put toward something. Sometimes our willingness to just do the work will lead us to identify our calling or bring us closer to realizing our dream. The work is hard, and it takes time. There are no shortcuts, but playing the long game, putting in the time, and earning your stripes makes others take notice and often pays off in big, unforeseen ways.

I'm talking to every single person when I say shortcuts will never pay the dividends that come from hard work. When I was an academic counselor, every season I always had one athlete (sometimes two or three) who didn't think I was talking to him. I would stand in front of the EMCC team in an academic meeting and go over (and over) what needed to be done to maintain eligibility. Then I would hear weeks or months into the season: "Oops! I didn't know you were talking to me."

The very first year I was a junior college counselor, we only had about five football players who received Division I scholarship offers. We were down to finals week, and all five players' grades were where they needed to be. *Whew!* I thought. *I made it through my first year with no major catastrophes.* But I was mistaken.

On the first day of finals my phone rang. A professor was calling to tell me my star linebacker hadn't shown up to take his final exam. I was shocked. His lowest grade going into final exams had been a C. If he showed up and did poorly on his exam, he would still be eligible to transfer to a Division I school. I called him. No answer. Coach called him. No answer. Hours later when we finally reached him, we discovered he'd gone home. He'd left campus without taking a single exam. He thought because his grades were okay, he didn't need to take his finals. He had moved on to celebrating the outcome before it had been secured. He thought he'd found a "shortcut."

The player got zeros on all his final exams, which caused him to flunk his classes. His eligibility blew up in his face.

Shortcuts cut dreams short.

For most of the athletes I have known, hard work is the key to their success. Raw talent only takes them so far. Very few athletes rise to greatness on talent alone. Even those freak athletes with incredible abilities must work hard at some point to hold on to their success. When talent begins to fade, the willingness to work becomes the separating factor. Tom Brady was seventh on the depth chart in college and the 199th selection of the NFL draft. The celebrated quarterback who has led his team to seven Super Bowl wins worked his way to greatness—the most recent of which was at the unlikely age of forty-three.

The higher we climb, the better the competition will be. Once you reach a certain level, everyone is "good." But the ones who put in the work, day in, day out separate themselves from the pack. Dreams can motivate and inspire, but hard work gets the job done.

Go with the Flow

Hard work is key to turning big dreams into reality, but another important factor is adaptability. I don't know a single person who chased a dream and had everything go according to plan. Adaptability is required to regroup and keep going when our goals get derailed. Charles Darwin once said: "It is not the strongest of the species that survives, nor the most intelligent that survives. It is the one that is most adaptable to change."

When circumstances and situations change, our dreams need to change also. We may start out on a path with one vision and then, along the way, the path bends and the vision blurs. When that vision comes back into focus, our dream looks different. It is our ability to adapt (or not) that either ignites or douses the flame.

As I mentioned in Chapter 9, the most ineffective saying in business and life is: "It's just the way we have always done it." I don't know who originated this statement, but I can picture him with his arms crossed, resolute on his path to irrelevancy. The year 2020 was a case study in adaptation. With national and global quarantines and travel bans, businesses had to find new ways of doing things or go under.

For example, think about public education. Teachers and students (and parents) across the nation were forced to change up teaching methods and philosophies they have used for years. It was amazing to watch schools and educators quickly respond with creativity and ingenuity. Within weeks, entire schools had switched to a completely virtual format. Teachers met with their classrooms over a computer.

These methods were borne out of necessity. The schools had to adapt or lose all usefulness. The pandemic magnified the digital divide between low-income and higher-income families, and school administrators had to find workarounds to quickly try to level the playing field. In Alabama, one school district wired school buses with

Wi-Fi and drove them to neighborhoods with little to no connectivity. This way children could sit close enough to the bus to have Internet access on school-provided Chromebooks. Others handed out bagged lunches instead of serving it in school cafeterias. At one point, my daughter ran a timed mile around our neighborhood to complete her PE test for the week.

Being forced to adapt stretches the limits of what we believe we can or cannot do. When we lean into change and have a willingness to discover new ways of doing things, we become better educators, better students, better parents, better bosses, and better employees. When we create new options and explore their use, we can identify not only *when* change is necessary, but *why* it's necessary.

Finding ways to adapt when life doesn't go as planned is imperative to keeping our dreams big. But what about the person who doesn't feel like they even have a dream? Just like me, with my self-doubts and trepidations during my college visits my junior year of high school, some people haven't seen enough or experienced enough to have a concrete dream, or the vision to see beyond their boundaries. This was the case with some of the athletes I worked with. Many of them had never been out of the city where they grew up. They had no conception of a better life because they hadn't seen enough to know what a better life would look like. This is a dismal reality that keeps certain populations in a downward spiral of poverty, crime, and despair.

I was in Philadelphia several years ago, where I met a ten-year-old boy who had been kicked out of his public school for behavioral issues and was attending an alternative school. His father was a drug lord, his mother was absent, and he lived in a drug house. Everyone the boy knew had either died or been in prison. He spent about fifteen minutes explaining to me how to escape the Philadelphia Penitentiary. I asked him why he thought I was going to prison (and therefore would need an escape plan). His response: "Everybody goes to prison."

He didn't have a dream because he hadn't seen enough beyond his world to dream. He and everyone around him seemed destined for prison. How could he imagine something different?

Some of us need to be shown what a dream looks like. We need to be inspired. We need to be taught how to create a better life. The reality is that we only know what we know and, by extension, we dream what we know. But dreaming what you already know limits you to what you have immediate access to.

Dreams can break cycles. They can break cycles of poverty, drugs, crime, ignorance, and oppression. I've seen it happen! When we realize that we have options and we can aspire to achieve those options, our priorities shift. Education becomes important. We pay attention and put forth effort in school. Promotions become goals, and we start showing up early and staying late. Knowledge becomes power, and we step outside our city or town, county, or state. We open our eyes to what others see, believe, and have become. We realize that relationships matter, and we remember to value them and to love one another.

Dreams don't care where you came from. They don't care what gender or race you are. They don't care what side of the street you stand on. Dreams are valid regardless of the labels placed on you. This is why diversity and representation are vital. It is important for all of us to see ourselves represented in the professional ladders we want to climb. From TV shows to businesses to the White House, it is imperative that we strive for representation and equity for everyone, especially those who have been historically and systemically underrepresented.

My junior year of college, I walked in the advisor's office still without a chosen major. I had no idea what I wanted to do with my life. This is the year when students have typically completed their general education and core classes, as I had done, and need to start narrowing their focus with an cyc toward graduation. My advisor told me I needed to choose a major. She handed me a course catalog and instructed me to figure it out—*now*. I flipped through the catalog and found the major with the least amount of math: sport communication. Sport communication required one math course beyond college algebra. *That was it!* This will be my major.

My advisor raised an eyebrow and asked, "Are you sure?" I wasn't sure about anything. She went on to explain that women didn't really work in athletics. In fact, statistically speaking, the odds that I would succeed in the field were dismal. Women such as sportscaster Erin Andrews hadn't risen through the ranks yet. Very few women were fighting to establish careers in areas such as sports journalism and other communications positions within professional athletics. At the time, I had to choose my field blindly. But today there are multiple examples of women in these fields who have broken barriers, allowing others to dream big.

On the National Portrait Gallery page of the Smithsonian website, Michelle Obama talks about the significance of her White House portrait:

> I'm thinking about all the young people, particularly girls and girls of color, who in years ahead will come to this place, and they will look up and they will see an image of someone who looks like them hanging on the wall of this great American institution. I know the kind of impact that will have on their lives because I was one of those girls.

You can climb the ladder that those who came before you have also climbed. And when there is no ladder, build your own. Carry it to a new spot, take one step at a time, and climb. Don't let anyone tell you it is not your ladder to climb. You are so much more than labels others place on you and what those labels may tell you about what you can or cannot achieve. Be proud of yourself and where you have been. Be determined to get where you are going. Be flexible in the road you take to get there. Hold your head up high and be proud of your dream because you are blazing a trail for others!

Sharpen Up!

Get rid of self-doubt you hold onto from labels, insecurities, or fears. Make a list of the labels that are holding you back. By acknowledging the labels that limit us, we start to strip away their power. Try this exercise: For a month, wear a rubber band around your wrist and any time limiting thoughts, words, or behaviors creep out, snap the rubber band and flip the limit to a possibility. Instead of saying, "I'm just a Mississippi girl," say, "Growing up in Mississippi gave me empathy for people and helped me see what I want out of life." Speaking the dream instead of the label will help to form a new belief. Don't squash your dreams; believe in your ability to accomplish them.

Dream hard, work hard. Shortcuts cut dreams short. Hard work is required when developing dreams. Make a list of the actions needed to accomplish a goal. Go to the top of that list and double the actions. For two weeks do double the work. Then evaluate the payoff of working a little bit harder. For example, on that journey to getting fit—work out six days a week instead of three. If you're trying to pay off debt, pay $100 instead of $50. If you need to reach out to two potential investors, reach out to four. Stretch yourself to work harder for just two weeks and create small successes and momentum you can celebrate.

Learn to adapt. Dreaming big requires finding ways to bounce back and move forward when adversity hits—to pause and breathe. (Remember the concept of "sit and hold" from Chapter 7.) Ask yourself what you can learn from this challenge. Look beyond the adversity and find the opportunities. Most importantly, remind yourself of why you set out in pursuit of this dream in the first place. Allow the *why* to motivate you.

Be a trailblazer. If you have the privilege of realizing your dream, help someone else see theirs! In helping others to realize and pursue their own dreams, I am motivated to work harder toward my own. When your motivation starts to diminish, look outward. Find someone to mentor, encourage, or help. I can guarantee that helping others will light your spark and reinvigorate your own dream.

Keep climbing and don't give up. The road to your next chance will not always be easy or go the way you expect it to. The key is to keep going—one step, one day, one goal at a time. While you are climbing, pause and enjoy the view. Offer yourself grace when you are tired and pat yourself on the back for how far you have come. Then continue to climb!

CHAPTER 11
Never Give Up

"Our greatest weakness lies in giving up.
The most certain way to succeed is always
to try just one more time."
—THOMAS EDISON

California has earthquakes. Colorado has blizzards. Florida has hurricanes. And Mississippi? We have tornados—and I have heard way too many tornado warning sirens.

I was in my office at EMCC in the middle of the afternoon when the Kemper County tornado siren blared. I hadn't noticed the sky darkening outside my window. The lights flickered and then the building went dark. This was definitely not a drill. Teachers, administrators, and staff began herding students into the interior hallway of the main academic building and looking for more people to usher to a safe place.

I saw a young man sitting in the hallway with a small light next to him. Was that Jimmie Gibson, the star linebacker on our team?

With Jimmie Gibson, the EMCC star linebacker who could teach all of us a lesson in perseverance.

As I got closer I could see him with a candle, a piece of paper, and a pencil, hunched over and writing.

"Jimmie, what are you doing?" I called down the hallway.

"I was in tutoring, Ms. Wagner, and now I want to finish this paper." I explained that we were in the middle of a tornado warning and I needed him to stop and move to a safer space in the building.

"I'm going to sit here and finish this until I get it right—tornado or not."

I spent most of my days begging these athletes to focus on academic work, but that day I was begging one of them to stop. As a tornado ripped through our town, Jimmie concentrated on finishing his paper.

While his timing was off, Jimmie's attitude of perseverance was admirable. In fact, I could learn something from him. I have been guilty of wasting time and making excuses. I imagine we all do this, at one point or another. Those who have an excuse and refuse to use it are the real winners—the ones who keep going when we wouldn't blame them for stopping.

Yes, You Can!

Years later, I traveled to Grandfalls, Texas, to be a motivational speaker and consultant at a high school. My goal was to inspire the faculty and staff to go above and beyond for their students, and listen to and encourage the students to keep going in education and life —even when their surroundings didn't offer them much opportunity. Grandfalls, Texas, is a tiny town forty miles outside Odessa with a population of about 400. The only thing separating Odessa from Grandfalls is miles and miles of rich oil fields. While these fields produce millions of dollars' worth of oil, the median income in Grandfalls is only $20,000 a year.

I fought back tears as I drove around the town and saw the living conditions of many of the students I was about to meet. They didn't have much; some didn't even have hot water or enough food to eat. There was no grocery store, police station, or public maintenance crew in the town.

Grandfalls' bright spot was its new high school building that rose up out of nowhere, a shiny fixture in a desolate landscape. The building itself was pretty, but the people inside were beautiful. I spent the day with the children, teachers, and staff at the school. I heard their stories of struggle and witnessed their smiles and enthusiasm. Most of the time, the high schoolers I meet are a tough audience. Not everyone wants to be there, no one wants to open up, and only half really listen. But not this group! These young female student athletes were smart, beautiful, and strong. They were hungry for inspiration and wisdom, and longing for someone to *see* them.

Grandfalls, like so many Texas towns, is known for its Friday Night Lights, and that year their football team had made it to the second round of the Texas high school playoffs. I was inspired by one player, in particular, though he wasn't on the high school team. His name was Nathan, and he was a middle school student with cerebral palsy. Nathan told me, smiling from ear to ear, that he had recently scored a touchdown at his school football game. Despite his disability, his parents had raised him with one rule. There were two words he wasn't allowed to say: "I can't."

With Nathan, the young man who does not know the word "no," in Grandfalls, Texas.

In a town where a student could easily say "I can't," and we wouldn't blame him, this young man, who had even more reason than most to discount himself, said, "I can!" Later that day, I saw the amazing video footage of Nathan crossing the goal line into the end zone. He started out midfield with his support crutches. About ten yards in, he dropped them and took off walking on his own down the field. Suddenly, his teammates swooped in, acting like human crutches and keeping him going. Then the wall of defenders on the opposing team opened up and began clapping. When he made it into the end zone, he turned to see his peers on the field celebrating his touchdown more than he celebrated it himself.

Nathan, his teammates, his coaches and teachers, and his town of Grandfalls shared a lesson we all need to learn. In an impoverished town less than a mile from the richest oil fields in America stands a young man who doesn't know the word "no," and who screams, "Yes, we can!"

Most people would look at Nathan and see a disability. They would look at Grandfalls, Texas, and see a lack of opportunity. How could a teen like Nathan have much hope of succeeding in life? I think all of us are constantly looking at our lives and situations and evaluating our chances of success. Sometimes, we use the seemingly negative strikes against us as an excuse not to try. We quit on a relationship because of how much damage there is to overcome. We walk away from a job because the ladder is too difficult and high to climb. We give up on a dream because *today* it seems overwhelming. However, if we broaden our perspective, we would see how many opportunities surround us every day. Our resources are rarely as limited as they feel. At first glance, Nathan's glass may appear half empty, but with community support and a positive attitude, he is holding the pitcher and can fill his glass anytime he wants. We are all holding our own pitcher.

Change Starts One Step at a Time

Don't misunderstand me; positive people have negative thoughts, too. They just don't focus on them or give them power. The secret lies in having the right perspective. When we see how far we have to go, or how many hurdles we have to cross, we can get bogged down and discouraged. In the midst of the "storm" we forget to pause and focus on what is directly in front of us. When we do that, we see a partner standing in front of us willing to do the work; we see the ladder and notice the fun we can have climbing to the top; we see that, yes, today achieving the dream seems impossible, but that could all change tomorrow.

But even with the right perspective, the goal in front of us will require effort. That's when refusing to allow negative thoughts to control us will help us mentally to forge ahead. Focusing on the potential opportunities instead of the obstacles helps us stay sane and inspires our self-confidence. Action is still required. Perspective does not cancel out the need for effort—sometimes thousands of hours of it.

You Can't Live Your Dream if You Don't Put in the Effort

The name of my company is 10 Thousand Pencils (10KP) for a specific reason. In his book *Outliers*, author Malcolm Gladwell presents the concept of 10,000 hours of effort. He teaches that it takes 10,000 hours for a person to master a skill. The difference between an "overnight" success (there are none, really) and the other guy is not necessarily raw talent but time put in, among other circumstances. The challenge is we often give up, believing that we aren't good enough and never will be. How many people have given up at hour 9,000? How many have quit just short of the reward?

My own consulting company and second chance—10KP—is a reflection of hours of effort and investment. I started out not knowing who I was or what I wanted to be. Self-doubt and insecurities plagued me. I hindered my own success and dreams because of where I came from—Mississippi—and the fact that I was a woman in a male-dominated career field. I have spent too many days pouring effort into unhealthy relationships that would ultimately fail instead of pouring into people who had already proven their staying power.

My company was formed after fifteen years of strenuous and often thankless work for colleges, coaches, and athletes. I formed it on my bedroom floor with a whole lot of questions and only a few answers. The difference in my first, second, and third chances are my own growth and effort—10,000 hours of it. During those hours of work, I discovered who I was, and I embraced my identity. I loved and allowed myself to be loved.

All my clients aren't success stories, but some are. And for the others, I gave it my all and planted a seed. Though it has been discouraging work at times, I have never given up. I have chosen to fight. Embracing my next chance for success has not always gone according to plan. I certainly don't have it all figured out. But I know my value and the rewards that come when I keep going. You have value, too, and you can also experience the rewards of not quitting.

In a video on YouTube, award-winning singer-songwriter Ed Sheeran reinforces this idea of the 10,000 hours through his own experiences. The musician downplays natural talent as the key to his success. In the video, he plays an audio recording of himself as a young musician singing a self-written song. In the audio clip, both Sheeran's voice and the song are terrible.

To improve his musical skills, he began writing two to five songs a day and playing multiple gigs a week. He did that for years until he finally wrote a hit song and played a memorable gig. The year he signed with Atlantic Records, he took the "yearly diary" of fellow singer-songwriter James Blunt—the record of the writing and

performances the musician had put in—and sought to double what
Blunt had produced. Sheeran's own "yearly diary" paid off, launching
him into his breakout year. He'd finally made it—on his ten thousandth hour of effort. I am not sure how many athletes I've worked
with or pencils I've handed out, but I keep telling myself to just keep
going because the ten thousandth one is right around the corner.

Self-Care Is Not Selfish

This kind of effort can be exhausting. At times it can feel draining,
hopeless, or just too much to conquer. A knife that is used over and
over becomes dull. Every thousandth cut, it needs to be resharpened.
That's when we stop cutting and tend to the tool to prepare it for its
next round of work. In our second chances, we are the tool. From time
to time, we need to be resharpened and rejuvenated. Self-care is not
optional, it is imperative when we are pursuing a long-term goal.

My twelve-year-old daughter thinks that pajama shorts, oversized
T-shirts, and Birkenstocks are appropriate attire for any occasion
or outing. I was beginning to think she didn't care much about her
appearance—until I took her shopping. Because of the coronavirus pandemic, she could not use a dressing room in the department
store (which I'm not allowed to enter with her during normal times).
Instead, we took the clothes home, and I got to see her try on the new
clothes and look at herself in the mirror.

I was amazed. Her eyes widened, and I could see her self-confidence
rise as she admired herself in clothes that made her feel attractive. Her
shoulders went back as she stood taller and examined her cuteness
from every angle. In those seconds of watching her feel beautiful, I
realized how important self-care is, even for adolescents.

We focus on what other people think about us, but our true

confidence and self-esteem comes from what we think about ourselves. Other people cannot build or break our confidence the way we can. I like to think of self-care as the wicker basket that we leave empty. It's the last item we tend to fill up—and often only if we have leftover time and energy. We give and give and give to others but neglect ourselves. Self-care is giving to and investing in ourselves. In truth, you make yourself *more available* to others if you take care of yourself first. Society can send the message that self-care is frivolous or selfish, but the truth is that self-care is vital.

What constitutes self-care is different for every person. Some examples are exercising, spending time alone, a night out with friends, a pedicure or massage, or even just a day of doing nothing. Sometimes self-care is saying "yes" and other times it's saying "no."

Women (and men, too) are notorious for neglecting self-care. We may think of it as nonessential or even selfish. But investing in our physical and mental health—taking the time to sharpen that tool for the task ahead—equips us to give to others in a more meaningful way. When the gas tank is empty, the car won't function. People are no different. We cannot show up for anyone else when we don't show up for ourselves. It may have been a long time since you've exercised the right to self-care, defined as "the practice of taking an active role in protecting one's own well-being and happiness, in particular during periods of stress." A key to moving forward is being proactive about caring for yourself.

According to the National Alliance on Mental Illness, "Caregivers who pay attention to their own physical and emotional health are better able to handle the challenges of supporting someone with mental illness. They adapt to changes, build strong relationships and recover from setbacks."

And the Office of Disease Prevention and Health Promotion classifies mental disorders as the leading cause of disability. They report that in any given year, 43.6 million Americans over the age of eighteen will suffer from a mental illness. A report by the CDC found that during the COVID-19 pandemic, those exhibiting symptoms of anxiety disorder were three times higher than the numbers reported in 2019. Forty-five percent of American college students believe they are under a higher-than-average stress level, according to a 2020 article written by Imed Bouchrika and published on *Guide2Research.com*. That same article shares that 61 percent of middle schoolers feel pressure to make good grades while 29 percent feel pressure to look good.

You are your greatest asset. Your physical and mental health is imperative to embracing your second chances. You need to take care of yourself in order to have the energy and fortitude to keep going. Keeping the right perspective, putting in the effort, and practicing regular self-care are essential elements in achieving success. There is no magic wand to make our dreams a reality (no matter how much we may wish there was).

Where, Exactly, Is the Magic Wand?

I grew up with Disney movies that all seemed to share a common story arc. A young woman encounters a challenge and is ultimately saved by a fairy godmother, a magic wand, or a prince. Early in my life, I was subconsciously waiting for all three to arrive. Well, maybe not a fairy godmother or magic wand, exactly, but some fortunate circumstance or ready-made opportunity to be handed over by a benevolent soul. I wish someone would have told me that waiting on someone else to step in and rescue me hindered what I could accomplish if I just put effort into my dream.

As an academic counselor, I saw many talented young people waiting on someone else to wave a magic wand to make their dreams happen. Even the most talented athletes often lacked self-confidence. Their inner monologue would whisper, *You aren't good enough to save yourself.* I was exhausted with their belief that I could somehow wave a magic wand and save them from their situation, academic trouble, or weak work ethic. I routinely asked athletes to scour my desk and tear it apart until they found my wand.

"Go through every drawer and find the thing," I would say.

They took me up on my challenge and looked. They would find Cheetos and pencils and Wite-Out. When everything was on the floor and the desk drawers were empty, they responded: "There is no magic wand."

Correct. I don't have one. No coach, mentor, soul mate, boss, friend, enemy, investor, teacher, therapist, social worker, president, or parent has one. The spiritual teacher Adyashanti puts it this way:

I got here by choice, by choice, by choice. If someone else was fully to blame then I have no hope because I don't have the ability to change anything that happens. I'm stuck. That is hopelessness! But when we realize there may be a link to someone else but we are ultimately responsible for the many things that we don't want to own up to, it is very liberating. The keys to happiness are in your own pocket.

Our lives are not someone else's responsibility, and thank the good Lord for that! No one else has the magic wand: You do. And what a glorious day it is when we awaken to the empowerment that lies in taking control of our own destiny. We still need the help of others, of course. Think about that middle school athlete with cerebral palsy. I will never forget Nathan and his big smile and unrelenting enthusiasm. Even with limitations, Nathan believed he could, and he did. But he did it with the help of his family and friends.

Eventually I did the same. *Last Chance U* created an opportunity and platform for which I am grateful. The biggest lesson I have learned from that experience is that there is no magic wand. There is no "easy" button. There is no big break that will instantly propel someone to success. The thing that catapults an individual to lasting success is hard work and showing up day after day. Persistent effort that is motivated by believing in oneself breaks down barriers, overcomes obstacles, and leads to an infinite number of next chances.

Platforms come in all shapes and sizes. Thousands of athletes are given the opportunity to play their sports at a competitive level, and yet few of them become a Big Ten or NFL success story. There are many "winners" of TV singing competitions, yet few go on to be chart-topping artists. Companies hand out platforms on a regular basis through promotions and illustrious positions and job titles, but a title alone doesn't earn the Fortune 500 stature. Platforms don't create success—people do.

If you are reading this book, then you woke up today with a platform. That platform may not be sexy or eye-catching, but it's there. Today you have an opportunity to use it to step into your next chance. You can do that by showing up for your life, pushing through your doubts and fears, and preparing to seize each opportunity that comes your way. As you walk (or run) toward what life has for you, remember that you are greater than your worst mistake. Erase it, make it right, and move on. If I were standing there with you now, I would hand you a pencil and tell you to use it.

For goodness' sake, be sure someone likes ya! Kindness doesn't cost you anything. In the moments where life—and your pain—feels too great and overwhelming, hold on and breathe—it'll pass. As you evolve and grow into a stronger version of yourself, be the solution for those around you. Dream big every day and dare to believe the absolute best for yourself. As you put forth genuine effort, in 10,000 ways big and small, give it your best. And, my friend, no matter what life hands you—believe in your worth and never give up. That is the beauty of chances; they are entirely dependent on you. Everything you need to change and grow already exists in you. The one person you must never give up on is *you*.

Recommended Reading

The 5 Love Languages: The Secret to Love that Lasts by Gary Chapman

Beating Anxiety & Depression for Life: Brain and Body Techniques that Work by Alison Buehler, Buddy Wagner, and Lynn Peterson

Daring Greatly: How the Courage to Be Vulnerable Transforms the Way We Live, Love, Parent, and Lead by Brené Brown

The Energy Bus: 10 Rules to Fuel Your Life, Work, and Team with Positive Energy by Jon Gordon

Fear Is a Choice: Tackling Life's Challenges with Dignity, Faith, and Determination by James Conner

A Million Little Pieces by James Frey

The Miracle Morning: The Not-So-Obvious Secret Guaranteed to Transform Your Life by Hal Elrod

Outliers: The Story of Success by Malcolm Gladwell

The Power of Now: A Guide to Spiritual Enlightenment by Eckhart Tolle

Rising Strong: How the Ability to Reset Transforms the Way We Live, Love, Parent, and Lead by Brené Brown

Start with Why: How Great Leaders Inspire Everyone to Take Action by Simon Sinek

The Subtle Art of Not Giving a F*ck: A Counterintuitive Approach to Living a Good Life by Mark Manson

Teaching with Poverty in Mind: What Being Poor Does to Kids' Brains and What Schools Can Do About It by Eric Jensen

Untamed by Glennon Doyle

What Happened to You? Conversations on Trauma, Resilience and Healing by Oprah Winfrey and Bruce D. Perry

You Are a Badass: How to Stop Doubting Your Greatness and Start Living an Awesome Life by Jen Sincero

About the Author

Brittany **Wagner** is a nationally respected athletic academic counselor and motivational speaker best known for her role as the breakout star of the hit Netflix documentary series, *Last Chance U*. Recognized for her compassion, encouragement, and no-nonsense attitude, Brittany guided many young men to academic and professional success despite run-ins with the law, extreme poverty, abandonment, and often a complete lack of academic preparedness. She has helped over 200 football players academically qualify for nationally respected NCAA Division I schools, and all the students Brittany advised who are currently playing in the NFL also hold college degrees.

Brittany's inadvertent stardom led to feature interviews with ABC's *Nightline,* the *Dan Patrick Show, GQ,* the *New York Times,* and *Sports Illustrated*—to name a few.

For the past four years, Brittany has traveled all over the country as a motivational speaker. In the fall of 2017, she launched her own company, 10 Thousand Pencils (10KP). Through 10KP, she is able to aid at-risk youth by working individually with high school and college-level administrators, counselors, and teachers to help them build relationships with these students and better support their emotional, social, and academic needs.

Brittany is an adjunct professor in the Stephens College of Business on the campus of the University of Montevallo. She also is a boxing coach at the boxing fitness club, Battle Republic.

Spectrum Originals optioned Brittany's life rights and is creating a new, scripted television series based on her personal and professional life as an athletic academic counselor. Actress Courteney Cox will be portraying Ms. Wagner in this series. Michael Strahan, Cox, and Wagner are all executive producers on the project.

Brittany earned both her undergraduate and graduate degrees in Sports Communication and Administration from Mississippi State University. She currently resides in Birmingham, Alabama, with her daughter, Kennedy, and dog, Ollie.

Hire Brittany for speaking engagements and/or consulting gigs through her website: *www.brittanywagner.com*.

Be motivated by and connect with Brittany on social media:

Twitter: Brittany_MSgirl

Instagram: Brittany_MSgirl

Facebook Fan Page: Brittany Wagner